MAR 2 9 2006

Arthur Miller

surance! You can't eat the orange and throw the peel aw
were promises made across this desk! You mustn't tell

Writers and Their Works

Arthur Miller

RICHARD ANDERSEN

Marshall Cavendish
Benchmark
New York

For My Best Friends:
Flore, Bobby, Anna, and Brünnhilde

With special thanks to Stephen Marino,
professor of English at St. Francis College in
Brooklyn, New York, and president of
the Arthur Miller Society, for his expert
review of this manuscript.

Marshall Cavendish Benchmark
99 White Plains Road
Tarrytown, NY 10591
www.marshallcavendish.us

All Internet sites were available and accurate when sent to press.

Library of Congress Cataloging-in-Publication Data
Andersen, Richard, 1946-
Arthur Miller / by Richard Andersen.— 1st ed.
p. cm. — (Writers and their works)
Summary: "A biography of writer Arthur Miller that describes his era, his
major works, his life, and the legacy of his writing"—Provided by publisher.
Includes bibliographical references and index.
ISBN 0-7614-1946-2
1. Miller, Arthur, 1915- 2. Dramatists, American—20th century—Biography. I. Title. II. Series.
PS3525.I5156Z513 2005
812'.52—dc22 2004023445

Photo research by Linda Sykes Picture Research, Hilton Head, SC

Cover: AP/Wide World

AP/ Wide World: 2; The Granger Collection: 8, 10, 37, 44; Bettmann/Corbis: 13, 21, 25, 78; Tina
Feinberg/AP Wide World: 28, 38; Elliott Erwitt/Magnum Photos: 19, 30; United Artists/ Seven Arts/ The
Kobal Collection: 31; Don Neiny/AP Wide World: 32; Bruce Davidson/Magnum Photos: 33; Dennis
Stock/Magnum Photos: 34; Adam Nadel/AP Wide World: 36; Inge Morath/Magnum Photos: 40;
Eric Y. Exit/ AP/Wide World: 48; (1996) Twentieth Century Fox: 87; Corbis-Sygma: 98.

Printed in China
1 3 5 6 4 2

Contents

ur years into this firm, Howard, and now I can't pay my
piece of fruit!I'm talking about your father! There were
e—I put thirty-four years into this firm, Howard, and r
way—a man is not a piece of fruit!I'm talking about you
ou've got people to see—I put thirty-four years into this
nd throw the peel away—a man is not a piece of fruit!I'm
ustn't tell me you've got people to see—I put thirty-four
t the orange and throw the peel away—a man is not a piec
his desk! You mustn't tell me you've got people to see—I pu
nce! You can't eat the orange and throw the peel away—a n
ses made across this desk! You mustn't tell me you've got
n't pay my insurance! You can't eat the orange and throw
here were promises made across this desk! You mustn't tell
nd now I can't pay my insurance! You can't eat the orange
our father! There were promises made across this desk! You
irm, Howard, and now I can't pay my insurance! You can't
alking about your father! There were promises made acros
ears into this firm, Howard, and now I can't pay my ins
iece of fruit!I'm talking about your father! There were p
put thirty-four years into this firm, Howard, and now I
man is not a piece of fruit!I'm talking about your fath
t people to see—I put thirty-four years into this firm,
hrow the peel away—a man is not a piece of fruit!I'm talki
't tell me you've got people to see—I put thirty-four year
he orange and throw the peel away—a man is not a piece
his desk! You mustn't tell me you've got people to see—I pu
nce! You can't eat the orange and throw the peel away—a n
ses made across this desk! You mustn't tell me you've got
n't pay my insurance! You can't eat the orange and throw
here were promises made across this desk! You mustn't tell
nd now I can't pay my insurance! You can't eat the orange
our father! There were promises made across this desk! You
irm, Howard, and now I can't pay my insurance! You can't
alking about your father! There were promises made acros
ears into this firm, Howard, and now I can't pay my ins
iece of fruit!I'm talking about your father! There were p
```
```

Part I:
How Arthur Miller
became ARTHUR MILLER

As a boy, Arthur Miller rode his bike to the boardwalk at Coney Island, in Brooklyn, New York, which was then and is now a popular bathing spot for Brooklyn residents.

Chapter 1

Becoming a Playwright

HE MOVED TO BROOKLYN. That was the start. He didn't have any choice. He'd been born in Manhattan on October 17, 1915, and spent the first thirteen years of his life growing up in a middle-class section of Harlem. Both his parents were Jewish immigrants from Eastern Europe. His father, Isidore, was a successful manufacturer of women's coats, and his mother, Augusta, taught school.

Miller didn't care much for school. In fact, he couldn't wait for classes to end each day so he could head to Central Park for pickup games of football and baseball. His favorite evenings were spent at the piano, and he wasn't the only one who could play. Sometimes the whole family—Miller has a sister Joan and a brother Kermit with whom he often competed for their father's attention—would gather around the piano to sing. He often refers to this time as "innocent."

Then it happened. The economy started to weaken, people started wearing last winter's coats, and it wasn't long before the Millers could no longer afford to live in Manhattan. They moved to a house in Brooklyn. Big elm trees stood at attention on both sides of East Third Street, the houses all had gardens, and Miller could bike to Coney Island to fish off the jetties.

Miller's house, which he later used as his model for the one in *Death of a Salesman*, wasn't as elegant as his home in Harlem, but it was a lot more active. His mom's father lived with them, and there always seemed to be a lot of people coming and going. Two of these—his uncles

ARTHUR MILLER'S LIFE WAS FOREVER CHANGED BY THE ECONOMIC DEPRESSION THAT HIT THE UNITED STATES IN THE 1930S. IT SHAPED HIS VIEWS OF SOCIETY, WHICH, IN TURN, COLORED THE VIEWS ESPOUSED IN HIS PLAYS. THIS FRONT PAGE HEADLINE IN *VARIETY*, THE MAIN NEWSPAPER OF THE THEATER TRADE, TRIES TO MAKE LIGHT OF AN EVENT WHICH THE NEWS STORY BENEATH IT RELATES AS "TRAGIC."

Manny Beigsby and Lee Balsam—were in sales. Miller listened to their tough talk and their complaints about the dog-eat-dog world they lived in, and from them he would one day create the most famous character in American theater history: Willy Loman.

But Miller wasn't thinking about writing at that time. He was too busy playing sports and—like Biff Loman—doing badly in math. Before graduating from Abraham Lincoln High School, he would fail algebra three times. When Miller won the Pulitzer Prize in 1949, no teacher remembered him as having been in one of his or her classes.

On October 23, 1929, Miller withdrew his life savings ($12) from the local bank to buy a used racing bike. The next day, the stock market crashed. Riding by his bank and seeing the crowd of people lined up in front of its gates with little hope of ever seeing their money again, he thought he'd beaten the Depression people said was soon to follow. A week later, he went into his house to get a glass of milk. When he came out, the bike was gone. As in *stolen* gone. It was the first serious lesson of his life: nobody escapes a world-class disaster.

Life for the Miller family quickly went from not so bad to not so good. The vegetable garden in the back of the house had to be expanded into the flowerbeds, and they raised rabbits and chickens to eat. Some of those relatives who used to complain about the savage practices of the business world were now unemployed and often on the verge of fainting from hunger. With little or no money being earned, pitching in and helping the family became more important than any family member's individual needs.

To want to go to a movie or even walk to Coney Island for a hot dog was seen as a betrayal of the family's collective effort to survive. Miller had to learn to use his hands for something other than shagging fly balls. He soon discovered he was good at working with tools. He built a porch on the back end of his family's house, and when he later bought a farm in Connecticut with the money he'd made from his first Broadway success, he constructed a cabin for writing and a small house for guests. He even did the plumbing.

Being good with his hands, however, didn't help Miller when he graduated from high school in 1932. He had his heart set on attending the University of Michigan, but his grades weren't good enough to get in, and even if he had been accepted, his family couldn't afford to pay the tuition. So he found whatever work he could: delivery boy for a bakery, dishwasher, crooner on a local radio station, and eventually, shipping clerk at an automobile parts warehouse in Manhattan. The warehouse became the setting for his one-act play *Memory of Two Mondays*, and like Bert in that play, Miller set aside $13 of his $15-a-week salary for tuition.

Working in Manhattan also meant riding the subway, and Miller quickly learned to do what many commuters do to escape the misery of their trips to and from the Big Apple: READ. He read more books in the two years he rode the subway than he had in his whole life. From the mental and emotional stimulation he experienced reading these books, Miller began imagining what it might be like to write one.

The problem was how to convince the people at the University of Michigan to give him a chance. After writing to the dean that he was now "a much more serious fellow," Miller was accepted by the School of Journalism in 1934 on the condition that he prove himself in his first year. It wouldn't be easy. He'd always done poorly in school, and though he had his tuition covered, he still had to work to support himself. While in Ann Arbor, his jobs included serving as the night clerk on the student newspaper and taking care of mice in one of the university's laboratories.

ARTHUR MILLER, LIKE SO MANY OTHER SUBWAY COMMUTERS, READ BOOKS
WHILE GOING TO AND FROM HIS JOB IN MANHATTAN.

Miller also met people in Ann Arbor who, like himself, were deeply affected by the Depression. They felt as if they'd been betrayed, as if the ideas they'd been taught by their parents and teachers of what it means to live in the land of opportunity had been an illusion. The real America wasn't streets paved with gold or even a chicken in every pot. It was executives jumping from skyscrapers, lawyers selling fruit on sidewalks, and people coming to the front door begging to wash windows in exchange for food.

The student to whom Miller was most drawn was Mary Grace Slattery. This highly principled, idealistic woman from Ohio made socialism, for Miller, more than a theory about which to tease his grandfather. Together they investigated, examined, and discussed ideas that could lead to change in America's economic structure and bring about real social progress for its people. They also believed they could directly influence the events that would make the American dream fit better with the American reality. They could, if they applied themselves, even create these events.

Miller created his first event during his second year at the University of Michigan after he saw an advertisement for a playwriting competition. He had seen two plays in his life and read three others and had to ask a friend how long an act should be, but none of that stopped him from cranking out *No Villain* in six days. The play is set in Brooklyn, concerns a family whose garment business is threatened by a financial crisis, and features two brothers who are in competition with each other for their father's affection. Sound familiar? Right from the beginning, Miller looked to his own experiences for the material that would help him articulate his social concerns. It turned out to be a good idea. He received the Hopwood Award of $250 and transferred to the English Department.

In Kenneth Rowe's playwriting class, Miller was introduced to the work of the Norwegian playwright Henrik

Ibsen. From Ibsen, he learned the importance of placing his concern with social issues in a good plot filled with realistic characters. What he didn't learn is what can happen to writers with strong social and political views. Like Ibsen, who got kicked out of Norway, they are often punished for questioning conventional ways of thinking.

While in Rowe's class, Miller revised *No Villain*, changed the title to *They Too Arise*, and won the Theatre Guild's Bureau of New Plays Award: $1,250. With *They Too Arise* on its way to productions in Ann Arbor and Detroit, Miller wrote *Honors at Dawn* and won his second Hopwood Award. This was also a play that concerns the relationship between two brothers, one of whom is hired by the corrupt administration of a university to spy on student radicals. When the second brother finds out, he leaves school, joins a union, and discovers a new level of social responsibility in the world of labor. Resolving family crises, coping with disillusion, and honoring the sense of personal integrity that can come through working with your hands: these themes thread their way through most of Miller's work and are a key to understanding what's important to him as a human being.

Miller didn't win the Hopwood Award in his final year at Michigan, but he did become engaged to Mary Slattery in 1938 and, after graduation, wasted no time in signing up for the Federal Theater Project in New York City, a government-sponsored relief agency that provided work for writers, actors, and technicians during the Depression. It didn't last long. Concerned about reports from the House Un-American Activities Committee that many of the people in the project had communist sympathies, Congress refused to renew funding for the agency. Miller's weekly salary of $22.77 came to an end after just a few months on the job.

Miller next tried his hand at radio plays. He wrote several half-hour scripts for "Cavalcade of America"

(National Broadcasting Corporation) and the "Columbia Workshop" (Columbia Broadcasting System) but learned to hate the restraints placed on him by producers. He was the one who had done all the work, yet they were the ones who had the power to make all the decisions.

In 1940, Miller married Mary and set up house in Brooklyn. While he worked at the Navy Yard during the day and labored on his plays in the evening, Mary took a job as a secretary in a Manhattan publishing house. Kept out of the military by a sports injury that never healed properly, Miller was once again making his living as a writer in 1944: he landed a job touring army camps for material on a movie called *The Story of GI Joe* about the famous war correspondent Ernie Pyle.

When his work was completed, Miller turned a journal he'd been keeping into a book that came out that same year. *Situation Normal* addresses some of the new ways soldiers who had been in combat now thought about war. It's a lot more about blood and guts than glory.

Still, Miller kept writing plays. He wrote about four or five between 1940 and 1943, but he didn't like any of them. Then he heard a story about a guy who was so successful that he started thinking people would try to rob him. Miller turned the story into an unpublished novel and later a play called *The Man Who Had All The Luck*. It tells the story of an auto mechanic for whom everything turns out amazingly well with very little effort on his part. Because he believes no single person deserves so much good luck, the man convinces himself that something bad is bound to happen. It's only a matter of time. A central conflict in the play is between two brothers who vie for the love of their father. *The Man Who Had All The Luck*, which was written as a serious drama, was produced as a comedy in 1944 and closed after only four performances.

Miller was so discouraged he wrote a novel. *Focus*, which was published in 1945 and produced as a film in 2001, is one of the first American novels to focus on anti-

Semitism. It looks at a man named Lawrence Newman, who becomes a New-man when he buys a pair of glasses and "looks Jewish" whenever he puts them on. Not only is he seen differently by others when he wears the glasses, he starts to see others differently as well. And whereas Newman never cared much about the anti-Semitic behavior he witnessed before he started wearing the glasses, by the novel's end he is ready to pick up a baseball bat to come to the aid of a neighborhood grocer who's being ostracized by his community because he is Jewish. Although much in the novel is overstated, *Focus* is important because it introduces what will become a major theme in Miller's plays: we are all responsible for what happens to each other.

In 1945, Miller's mother-in-law told him a story about a girl who denounced her father when she discovered he'd supplied defective engine parts to the army during World War II. Within a year, Miller turned the story into a play. *All My Sons* opened on Broadway in January of 1947, ran for 328 performances, won the Drama Critics Circle Award, was produced in Paris and Stockholm, and appeared as a film in 1948. In addition to the now familiar two competing brothers, *All My Sons* introduces a father whose capitalist values lead to his suicide when he's forced to accept responsibility for the role he played in the deaths of twenty-one aviators, the guilt-ridden suicide of his oldest son, and the imprisonment of his business partner. The play also features a mother who shields her husband but never herself from the truth. Two sons, a father whose false values lead to his downfall, and a mother who furthers an illusion: these characters reappear in a different context in Miller's next, best, and most important play: *Death of a Salesman.*

But Miller didn't immediately begin writing the work for which he'll always be known. For the first time since his bicycle was stolen he had some extra money, and he and his wife were busy spending it. They bought a house in

Brooklyn and a farm in Connecticut on which to raise their two kids: Jane (born in 1944) and Robert (1947). Miller also built a writing cabin on the farm and started working on a love story that a year later still hadn't heated up. Then, one evening, he remembered the two uncles who worked as salesmen for his father. This thought led to others and before the night was over, Miller had written two-thirds of a play. Nothing he'd written had ever come faster or easier.

It took Miller another six weeks to finish his play, but when it was produced on Broadway in 1949, *Death of a Salesman* catapulted Miller into the first rank of American writers. It ran for 742 performances and won the Antoinette Perry Award, the Drama Critics Circle Award, and the Pulitzer Prize for Best Play. It also spawned two road companies, was made into the first of several movies, was seen by millions on television, and became a standard for almost every repertory company in the country. High schools and colleges soon followed with productions of their own. It wouldn't be very long before *Death of a Salesman* was being performed in China, and today there is rarely a day when it isn't being performed somewhere in the world. The man who had all the luck was named "Outstanding Father of the Year" and even became acquainted with Marilyn Monroe, a young starlet who was soon to become one of Hollywood's biggest movie celebrities and the nation's top sex symbol.

With fame came blame. Many conservatives saw *Death of a Salesman* as an attack on capitalism, and Miller was forced to defend himself in magazine articles and newspaper interviews. His playwriting and his family life suffered as he was drawn more and more into the public spotlight. Unable to create a drama out of his own distracted imagination, he adapted for Broadway Henrik Ibsen's *An Enemy of the People*. Produced in 1950, this play features a man who is ridiculed by his community for threatening to go public with the news that the local health spa is polluted. It was seen by critics as an attack on liberals who

ARTHUR MILLER, ALREADY A FAMOUS PLAYWRIGHT, POSES ON THE CORNER OF DOUGHTY STREET IN NEW YORK AS IF HE WERE JUST "ANY" MAN, MAYBE EVEN WILLY LOMAN IN *DEATH OF A SALESMAN*.

were afraid to stand up to the rising tide of conservative public opinion in America.

Many of these liberals believed they had good reasons to keep low profiles. One of them was the House Un-American Activities Committee. Founded in 1938 to investigate the extent of communist infiltration in the United States, the HUAC was disbanded during World War II but came back with a vengeance in 1945 when the Soviet Union became America's Public Enemy No. 1. The HUAC won widespread public support in 1948 when it accused Alger Hiss, a high-ranking member of the State Department, of being a spy for the Soviet Union. He was convicted not of spying but of perjury, and his innocence is still being debated today.

> The trouble with literature is that writers have to be the ones to write it. It's always partial, it's always partisan, it's always incomplete . . . one has to be a species of fanatic. You have to think that it is really the only thing worth doing. Otherwise, you can't generate the intensity to do it well.
> —Arthur Miller

Almost anyone of influence who disagreed with Congress's decision to sacrifice its citizens' individual rights so the government could have more power in its Cold War against communism was considered unpatriotic and became a target of the HUAC. Opponents of the committee called its work a "witch hunt." Few of the people investigated by the committee were communists; nor were they a threat to the United States government.

This ugly footnote in American history is also an odd one. The committee summoned what it called "witnesses" to state what they knew about the extent of the commu-

PICTURED HERE ARE SEVEN HOLLYWOOD SCREENWRITERS ON THEIR WAY TO TESTIFY BEFORE THE HOUSE UN-AMERICAN ACTIVITIES COMMITTEE IN 1950. THEIR CAREERS WERE RUINED BECAUSE THEY REFUSED TO "NAME NAMES" OF PEOPLE SUSPECTED TO BE COMMUNIST.

nist influence where they lived and worked. These witnesses were not charged with any crimes, but neither were they given the same safeguards they would have been entitled to in a court of law. They could consult with lawyers, for example, but the lawyers couldn't speak on their behalf, and anything the witnesses said could be used to subpoena someone else. Everything that was said, whether it was based in fact or fiction, became part of the public record and anything that reinforced the notion of a communist threat was regarded as truth. Witnesses who claimed the First Amendment of the Constitution protected their right to free speech were perceived by the committee as communist sympathizers. Those who pleaded the Fifth Amendment, which says that citizens have the right not to say anything that will incriminate them, were made to look as if they were guilty or trying to hide something.

> To some extent an artist has to step to one side of what is happening, divorce himself from his role as a citizen, and in that sense he becomes the enemy because he does not carry forth in himself and believe what is being believed around him. He is the enemy usually, I suppose, of the way things are, what way they are.
>
> —Arthur Miller

That the hearings were televised only fanned the flames of public paranoia. Many Americans whose political views were at odds with those of the committee's members lost their jobs and were persecuted by the people where they lived. Some even committed suicide.

The words "witch hunt" struck a chord with Miller. He'd been fascinated with the seventeenth-century hunt for witches in Salem, Massachusetts, ever since he learned about them at the University of Michigan. Now he saw a parallel between those trials and the hearings taking place in Washington, D.C. In both instances, people were being harassed not only to admit something of which they may not have been guilty but to provide the names of fellow travelers as well.

What had fascinated Miller most about the trials in Salem, however, was how many people refused to admit to being witches or name anyone else as a witch when a simple confession—even if it was a lie and everyone knew it—was all anyone had to do to save his or her life. They'd rather die than lie under an oath made to God. Of course, no witness in Washington was threatened with death, but those who refused to name names could be charged with contempt, fined, and sentenced to jail.

Miller now had a subject from which nothing could distract him. Once he completed the research, *The Crucible* came out on paper almost as quickly as *Death of a Salesman*. The play won the Antoinette Perry and Donaldson Awards for Best Drama of 1953, and it didn't take a genius to connect Miller's play with the hearings in Washington. But press reviews were less than enthusiastic in spite of nineteen curtain calls at the opening night performance, and *The Crucible* closed within a few months. Reading those reviews today, it's obvious that many of the critics either believed the government's propaganda or were afraid to honestly examine a work that was so openly critical of the House Un-American Activities Committee. A common thread running through many of these reviews is the claim that whereas witches didn't exist, communism did.

When Miller applied for a passport to attend the play's Belgian premiere in 1954, the State Department denied his application, and when he began working on a play about street gangs for the Youth Board of New York in 1955, government agents informed the board it had employed a communist sympathizer. Miller had not only enrolled in a course on Marxism, he'd attended five writers meetings sponsored by the Communist Party in 1947. He also participated in world conferences for peace in Paris (1948) and New York (1949), and he'd more than once openly criticized the work of the HUAC. When organizations such as the American Legion and Catholic War Veterans protested that public funds were being used to support a man whose politics opposed the "war" on communism, Miller was fired.

Miller rebounded with two one-act dramas, *A View From the Bridge* and *A Memory of Two Mondays*, but when they opened on Broadway in September of 1955, the press reported government agents photographing people as they entered and left the theater. The double bill closed after only twenty performances to reviews that pictured Miller as a man whose talent had been used up. Stung by the harsh and often personal criticism and reeling

from the government's interference in his private and pro-
fessional life, Miller withered. He withdrew to the sereni-
ty of his farm in Connecticut but found little relief there.
His wife wasn't able to pull him out of his depression, and
when tension mounted between the two, he began seeing
more and more of Marilyn Monroe. By mid-1956, Miller
was divorced and living in Manhattan. Then, just to make
sure the American people thoroughly understood the message that had been sent to the Millers about what happens
to people who challenge those in power, the HUAC summoned Miller to Washington to assist in its investigation
into the improper use of passports.

The real reason for Miller's being subpoenaed, of course,
was not passports but to test in front of television cameras the
loyalty of a chastened celebrity whose name had become
increasingly linked with a Hollywood star. Then, on the
morning of his scheduled appearance, Miller was offered
the opportunity of having his subpoena withdrawn if he'd
convince Monroe to pose for a photograph with the chair of
the committee. Miller refused, and the committee decided to
play hardball. Miller and Monroe would keep the HUAC in
the news, and the news would make sure the government's
inflated threat of communism continued to hold a prominent
place in the nation's collective imagination.

Like *The Crucible*'s John Proctor, who implicates himself before his Puritan judges but refuses to point a finger
at anyone else, Miller admitted his leftist sympathies
before the HUAC but refused to name anyone who shared
his political convictions. The committee found him guilty
of contempt, fined him $500, and sentenced him to three
months in jail even though the committee already had the
two names of the people it wanted Miller to denounce and
thirteen other witnesses had refused to name names and
were not similarly convicted. The United States Court of

ARTHUR MILLER WAS ENGAGED TO MOVIE ACTRESS AND SEX SYMBOL MARILYN MONROE AT THE TIME OF HIS TESTIMONY BEFORE THE HOUSE UN-AMERICAN ACTIVITIES COMMITTEE. HERE, REPORTERS QUESTION HER ABOUT HER FIANCÉ'S TESTIMONY.

Appeals overturned the committee's ruling in 1958, but what hurt Miller most at the time of the hearing was the number of people who spoke out in his defense: NOT ONE. And some of those who'd denounced him as a communist—including the director of *Death of a Salesman*—were people he considered his friends.

When Arthur Miller and Marilyn Monroe met in 1950, Miller was considered America's greatest playwright and had been called "serious" and "an intellectual" by his critics. Monroe was eleven years younger. Frustrated with being portrayed as a sex goddess and not a talented actor, she enrolled in Lee Strasberg's school for serious actors in New York. At the time Monroe met Miller, she was still romantically involved with one of the most famous baseball players of all time: Joe DiMaggio. They were married in 1954 and divorced nine months later. Between 1950 and 1956, Miller's marriage soured—we get a glimpse of this deterioration in the tension that exists between John and Elizabeth Proctor in *The Crucible*—and he began seeing more and more of Monroe. Seventeen days after Miller divorced his wife in 1956, Miller and Monroe were married.

Within weeks of the wedding, the couple was off to England: she to star in a movie with Laurence Olivier; he to work with famed director Peter Brook on a two-act version of *A View From the Bridge*. But once they were in London, Miller started spending less time in the theater working on his play and more time on the set of his wife's movie. He soon found himself responding publicly to complaints about Monroe's chronic lateness, her showing up for work unprepared, her inability to remember lines, her impatience with others, and more. When he returned to New York to see his sick daughter, the 1949 "Outstanding Father of the Year" cut his visit short and flew back to London because Monroe was upset after discovering he had written something bad about her in a notebook.

Epithalamic Blues

Arthur was a writer, he had Left Wing traits;
He wrote *Death of a Salesman* and wowed them
    in the States.
So then he wrote another piece, obliquely named
    The Crucible,
And, politically speaking, it was almost unproducible.
Arthur sought a passport from his Uncle Sam,
And when he couldn't get it, he sure was in a jam—
But he knew
What to do
And so
He hauled off and married
Marilyn Monroe.
Yeah, he hauled off and married Marilyn Monroe!
Her fans stayed as faithful as before, or more so,
But turned their attention to her head from her torso,
While in every milk-bar and sports arcade
The hepcats sang this serenade:

"I'm just crazy over Mrs. Arthur Miller!
Mrs. Arthur Miller's my number one thriller.
With her new-style dumb-intellectual blend
She can show you how Timon is a girl's best friend.

"If her countrymen forget her real talent
    when she's dead
You can wager they'll remember her for
    something else instead
For she's a public hero of a one-time Red—
Mrs. Miller, the queen of them all!"
                      B.A.Y.

ACTRESS MARILYN MONROE AND ARTHUR MILLER EMBRACE ON THE LAWN OF MILLER'S HOME IN ROXBURY, CONNECTICUT, ON JUNE 29, 1956, HOURS BEFORE THEY WERE MARRIED. FIVE YEARS LATER, THEY WERE DIVORCED.

The following summer, the couple rented a house on Long Island; Miller describes this period as the happiest of their married life. She played at being a housewife, and they were soon looking forward to having a baby. Monroe had a miscarriage in the fall, and in an effort to take Monroe's mind off her loss, Miller vowed to write a screenplay with a serious role in it for her. In August of 1958, the two moved to Hollywood, where Monroe began work on the movie for which she is best known today: *Some Like It Hot*. She was again pregnant and again she miscarried, but this time her husband had his screenplay: *The Misfits*. Then, while Miller searched for shooting locations in Nevada with director John Huston, Monroe fell in love with the co-star of her next film: Yves Montand.

When Miller discovered the affair from stories in the press during the summer of 1960, his relationship with Monroe deteriorated rapidly. By January 1961 they were divorced, and a little more than a year later, Monroe was dead from an overdose of sleeping pills at the age of thirty-six. Although there was speculation that she'd been killed by the Central Intelligence Agency (CIA) because she was threatening to make public the affairs she'd had with President John F. Kennedy and his brother Robert, the rumors were never investigated.

Back in Connecticut, Miller tried to find some meaning in what had happened. Criticized by both wives for being emotionally distant, he confronted himself with the role he might have played in the collapse of his marriages. He also became romantically involved with Austrian-born Ingeborg Morath, a publicist for *The Misfits* who'd come on assignment to photograph Miller on his farm. Morath turned out to be just the person Miller needed to provide some stability in his life. They were married in 1962, and a daughter, Rebecca, was born a year later.

MARILYN MONROE POSES PRETTILY ON THE SET OF *THE MISFITS*, BUT SHE
WAS CHRONICALLY LATE TO THE SET AND FOREVER BLOWING HER LINES.

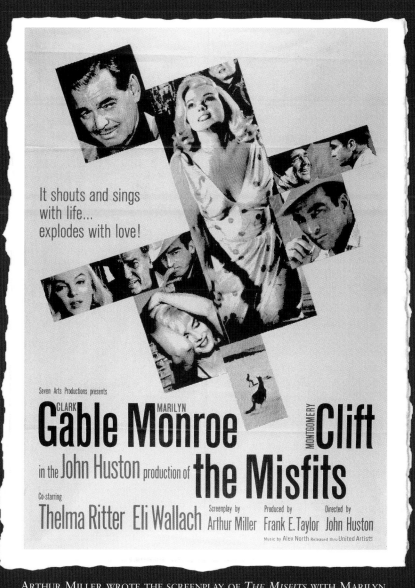

It shouts and sings with life... explodes with love!

Seven Arts Productions presents

CLARK
Gable MARILYN **Monroe** MONTGOMERY **Clift**

in the John Huston production of **the Misfits**

Co-starring

Thelma Ritter **Eli Wallach** Screenplay by Arthur Miller Produced by Frank E. Taylor Directed by John Huston

Music by Alex North Released thru United Artists

ARTHUR MILLER WROTE THE SCREENPLAY OF *THE MISFITS* WITH MARILYN MONROE SPECIFICALLY IN MIND.

A 1989 PHOTO OF INGE MORATH.

Finally able to work without the distractions of New York, Washington, and Hollywood, Miller wrote his first play in eight years. It was a disaster. Commissioned for the new Lincoln Center Repertory Theater, the play was appropriately titled *After the Fall* (1964). The characters Quentin and Maggie seem to parallel Miller's marriage with Monroe as obviously as his treatment of the witch hunts in Salem paralleled the HUAC hearings in Washington. Miller claimed the play was no more autobiographical than any of his other works, but the damage had been done. Critics viewed the play as an act of revenge done in bad taste, especially as it came so soon after

ARTHUR MILLER MARRIED HAPPILY THE THIRD TIME AROUND. HERE HE IS IN 1987 IN HIS HOME WITH HIS WIFE INGE MORATH AND DAUGHTER REBECCA.

Monroe's suicide. Nevertheless, Miller's fellow writers elected him president of the international literary organization Poets, Essayists, and Novelists (PEN), and from 1965 to 1969, he led a campaign on behalf of writers oppressed by totalitarian regimes.

He also wrote his last great Broadway success. *The Price* (1968), which ran for 425 performances in New York and for more than a year in London, continues many of the themes and conflicts presented so effectively in *Death of a Salesman*. Once again we have two troubled brothers and a failed father. While Victor became a policeman at a young age to support his father after he'd been

IN 1964, ARTHUR MILLER'S PLAY *AFTER THE FALL* OPENED AT THE
LINCOLN REPERTORY THEATER IN NEW YORK. IT WAS CONTROVERSIAL
BECAUSE OF ITS DEPICTION OF AN ACTRESS SUSPICIOUSLY SIMILAR TO
MARILYN MONROE, BUT IT HAS BEEN REVIVED MANY TIMES, MOST
RECENTLY IN 2004.

emotionally and economically crippled by the stock market crash of 1929, his older brother Walter left home to further his education and become a successful doctor. Victor prides himself on having assumed responsibility for their father, but he also regrets sacrificing a more personally satisfying career for an unappreciative man who always prized success over love. Walter, for his part, sees Victor's loyalty as a criticism of his own decision to protect himself from the economic ruin that wreaked such havoc on their father. Each brother, then, has paid a price: Victor's faithfulness to his father has prevented him from realizing his full potential, and Walter's guilt for not being responsible for his father has cost him his peace of mind.

Miller's preoccupation with brothers and their father is also the subject of his next Broadway play, but when *The Creation of the World and Other Business* appeared in 1972, it did not attract an audience. It closed after twenty performances. A revival of *The Price* in 1979 flopped after twelve nights, and the play that appeared in 1980, *The American Clock*, only lasted ten performances. Perhaps because of these failures, Miller began turning to other subjects, other genres, and theaters other than the ones found on Broadway.

And not without some success. *The Archbishop's Ceiling* (1977) lasted four weeks at the Kennedy Center in Washington, D.C. The following year, his one-act play *Fame* (1970) was made into a television drama, and another one-act play, *The Reason Why* (1970), appeared as a movie. *The Crucible* was produced as a play In 1996. His play *Broken Glass* (1994) won the Olivier Award for best new play on the London stage, and *The Crucible*, starring Liam Neeson, was revived on Broadway in 2002. *Incident at Vichy*, which ran for only twenty performances in New York in 1964, was produced on television in 1973. Television has also hosted performances of *All My*

PROMINENT JEWISH AMERICANS POSE FOR A PHOTO IN A MAZE ON ELLIS ISLAND, NEW YORK, WHICH WAS THE LANDING SPOT FOR MANY IMMIGRANTS TO THE UNITED STATES. FROM LEFT FRONT: ARTIST ROY LICHTENSTEIN; ACTRESS LAUREN BACALL; VIOLINIST ITZHAK PERLMAN; ARTHUR MILLER (CENTER, IN TAN COAT); SUPREME COURT JUSTICE RUTH BADER GINSBURG.

Sons (1987), his adaptation of Henrik Ibsen's *An Enemy of the People* (1990), *The American Clock* (1993), and four productions of *Death of a Salesman* (1950, 1966, 1985, 2000).

In addition to these adaptations of his plays, Miller has written the texts for three books featuring photographs by his wife, Inge Morath. *Playing for Time*, his original teleplay about how a Jewish cabaret singer named Fania

A POSTER FROM THE 1965 OPENING OF ARTHUR MILLER'S PLAY *A VIEW FROM THE BRIDGE*.

Fenelon survived the Nazi death camp at Auschwitz as a member of the prison orchestra was critically well received in 1980. The playwright's work has also inspired others. *The Creation of the World and Other Business* has been turned into a musical, *A View From the Bridge* has been performed as an opera, and Miller fans can see *The Crucible* as a movie, an opera, and even a ballet.

The fiftieth-anniversary production of *Death of a*

ARTHUR MILLER STANDS IN FRONT OF A STREET SIGN RENAMING WEST 49TH STREET BETWEEN BROADWAY AND EIGHTH AVENUE "ARTHUR MILLER WAY." THE UNVEILING WAS PART OF A CELEBRATION OF THE FIFTIETH ANNIVERSARY OF DEATH OF A SALESMAN, WHICH WAS REVIVED AT THE EUGENE O'NEILL THEATER IN NEW YORK ON FEBRUARY 10, 1999.

Salesman in 1999 marks the beginning of Miller's resurgence in the American theater. The play won three Tony Awards for Best Revival, Best Actor (Brian Dennehy), and Best Featured Actress (Elizabeth Franz), and at the same ceremony honoring his play, Miller received an award for Lifetime Achievement. After that, Miller premiered two plays—*Resurrection Blues* in 2002 and *Finishing the Picture* in 2004. Miller died February 10, 2005, at age eighty-nine. The cause was congestive heart failure.

Nothing that Miller wrote between 1954 and his death in 2005 equals the intellectual and artistic triumphs of *Death of a Salesman* in 1949 and *The Crucible* in 1953. They are the reason his stature as a playwright continues to soar while some of his more recent works have a hard time getting off the ground. In 1956, he was given an honorary doctorate at the University of Michigan; in 1958, he was awarded the Gold Medal for Drama by the National Institute of Arts and Letters; and in 1969, he was presented with the Brandeis University Creative Arts Medal. He has long been considered America's greatest playwright, and is likely to remain so regarded.

Death of a Salesman and *The Crucible* continue to be read in schools and produced in community theaters because they raise their audiences' levels of political and social awareness as much now as they did when they first appeared on Broadway. They serve as a standard by which to measure the effects on ordinary men and women of today's increase in corporate greed, the shortage of jobs, the growing gap between rich and poor, and the largest deficit in United States history. Arthur Miller was one of a handful of modern writers and artists representing the conscience of humanity; his works are a

THIS POSTER OF MILLER'S PLAY, *THE RIDE DOWN MT. MORGAN*, WHICH OPENED IN LONDON IN 1999, WAS CREATED BY INGE MORATH, MILLER'S THIRD WIFE.

first line of defense against the worsening of the human condition by those who wield power irresponsibly. And, as Linda Loman tells us in *Death of a Salesman*, "Attention must be paid."

hirty-four years into this firm, Howard, and now I can't
a man is not a piece of fruit! I'm talking about your fath
ou've got people to see—I put thirty-four years into this
range and throw the peel away—a man is not a piece of fr
his desk! You mustn't tell me you've got people to see—I
y insurance! You can't eat the orange and throw the peel
here were promises made across this desk! You mustn't tel
oward, and now I can't pay my insurance! You can't eat th
alking about your father! There were promises made acros
y-four years into this firm, Howard, and now I can't pay
an is not a piece of fruit! I'm talking about your fathe
ou've got people to see—I put thirty-four years into this
range and throw the peel away—a man is not a piece of fr
his desk! You mustn't tell me you've got people to see—I
y insurance! You can't eat the orange and throw the peel
here were promises made across this desk! You mustn't tel
oward, and now I can't pay my insurance! You can't eat th
alking about your father! There were promises made acros
y-four years into this firm, Howard, and now I can't pay
an is not a piece of fruit! I'm talking about your fathe
ou've got people to see—I put thirty-four years into this
range and throw the peel away—a man is not a piece of fr
his desk! You mustn't tell me you've got people to see—I
y insurance! You can't eat the orange and throw the peel
here were promises made across this desk! You mustn't tel
oward, and now I can't pay my insurance! You can't eat th
alking about your father! There were promises made acros
y-four years into this firm, Howard, and now I can't pay
an is not a piece of fruit! I'm talking about your fathe
ou've got people to see—I put thirty-four years into this
range and throw the peel away—a man is not a piece of fr
his desk! You mustn't tell me you've got people to see—I
y insurance! You can't eat the orange and throw the peel
here were promises made across this desk! You mustn't tel
oward, and now I can't pay my insurance! You can't eat th
alking about your father! There were promises made acros
y-four years into this firm, Howard, and now I can't pay

Part II:
Death of a Salesman

THIS POSTER FOR THE 1949 VERSION OF *DEATH OF A SALESMAN* PERFECTLY EVOKES THE WEARINESS OF WILLY LOMAN.

Chapter 1

Death of a Salesman—Setting the Scene

> You can't eat the orange and throw the
> peel away—a man is not a piece of fruit!
> Willy Loman

IMAGINE THAT IT'S OPENING NIGHT on Broadway. You have a ticket to *The Inside of His Head*, a new play by Arthur Miller. You take your seat and then you see it: a huge face painted on a screen that takes up almost the whole stage. The lights go down, the screen goes up, and the skeletal structure of a house appears. A frame for the roof is where the forehead on the face was, and there are two upstairs bedrooms in place of the eyes. Beneath one of the bedrooms is a kitchen, but like the roof, its walls aren't complete walls, but just the frames for walls.

A light comes on in the kitchen, and a tired man dragging two suitcases enters. His wife hears him, calls to him, and asks him how his day has been. It has not been good, to say the least. The light suddenly goes out and another light comes on in one of the upstairs bedrooms to reveal two brothers talking about their father in the kitchen below. Other events start taking place in and around the house. Some of these events take place in the present, and others take place in the past. The characters act like the walls are real when they are in present time and walk right through the walls when their actions occur in the past. After a while, it dawns on you: a lot of what is taking place in this play is occurring inside the head of the fellow who dragged in the suitcases. There's a word for this technique of making the psychological action of the play (what goes on inside

Willy's head) as real as any physical behavior. It's called "Expressionism."

This at first confusing but later revealing combination of the real and unreal is how Arthur Miller imagined *Death of a Salesman* when he first wrote it. But then he changed the title to what it's known as today. Why do you think he did that? Why tell everybody how your play is going to end before it begins? The producers thought it was a bad idea. *The Inside of His Head* wasn't the biggest attention-grabber they'd ever heard, but *Death of a Salesman*? It didn't sound like a fun night at the theater. And who would want to spend money to see a play about a salesman who dies?

Miller argued that calling the play *Death of a Salesman* would shift the audience's attention from guessing *what* was going to happen to trying to understand the reasons *why* it happened. These reasons, now more evident to audiences because they already knew the outcome of the play, examine and explain the human condition as Miller viewed it in twentieth-century America. Let's look closer at Willy Loman and the other characters in the play to see what we can learn about them, ourselves, and the time in which we live.

Chapter 2

The Characters

Willy Loman

WILLY LOMAN HAS TWO DESIRES: to be successful and to be "well liked." He got the first idea from his big brother Ben, who, Willy says, went into the jungle at the age of seventeen and came out a rich man when he was only twenty-one. The second idea came from Dave Singleman, a salesman who was so beloved his funeral was attended by more people than Willy probably knows. When we meet Willy dragging into the kitchen the suitcases containing the merchandise he tries to sell, Willy is neither successful nor liked. We also discover he's recently been in a few car accidents that haven't exactly been accidental. An eyewitness to his latest mishap has reported that he wasn't going as fast as he said, didn't skid as he claimed, and intentionally smashed into the railing of a bridge. Only the shallowness of the water prevented him from drowning.

Willy's brother Ben, who is dead when the play begins, was a success in the sense that he made a lot of money. Something of a romantic, almost mythic adventurer in Willy's mind, Ben was a conqueror in the world of competition, exploitation, and greed. Willy can't tell us exactly how Ben made his millions in the African diamond industry, but we know from his treatment of Willy's son Biff that he doesn't hesitate to be violent or play unfairly. Because Willy hasn't had the courage to take the kinds of risks he believes made his brother rich, he tries to pass Ben's values onto Biff and his other son, Happy. When we meet them, both men have been athletes: Biff was the captain of his high school football team, and Happy claims he can

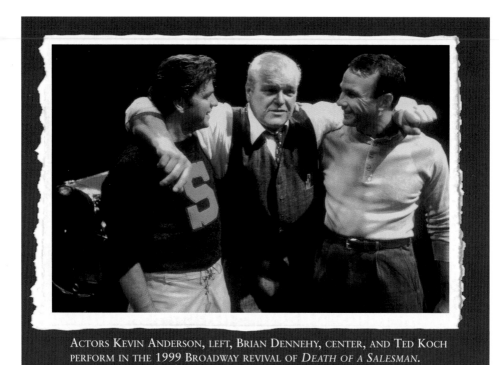

ACTORS KEVIN ANDERSON, LEFT, BRIAN DENNEHY, CENTER, AND TED KOCH
PERFORM IN THE 1999 BROADWAY REVIVAL OF *DEATH OF A SALESMAN*.

still box well enough to clobber anyone in the office where
he now works. But neither has developed a sense of fair
play: Biff has spent three months in jail for larceny before
returning home, and Happy has seduced the fiancées of
three of his bosses.

Dave Singleman, Willy's other role model, was such a
successful salesman he could make all his calls without
ever having to leave his hotel room. And he was still going
strong at the age of eighty-four. When Dave died, hundreds of his former customers attended the funeral
because they were so fond of him. Willy wants to be
appreciated in the same way that he imagines this singu-
lar man to be, but because he isn't, he coaches his sons on
how he thinks they need to behave to be successful like
Dave. "The man who makes an appearance in the business world," Willy tells Biff and Happy, "is the man who
gets ahead. Be liked and you will never want." What every
successful salesperson knows and Willy never realizes, is

that Dave's customers didn't buy from him because they liked him; they bought from him because of what he sold, the price at which he sold it, and the services he provided before and after the sale was made. It is only in the course of these exchanges that they came to know him and like him as a person. In other words, Willy has put his cart before his horse and then failed to figure out why he never arrived where he wanted to go.

Like Ben and Dave, Willy believes in the American Dream of equal opportunity to succeed. But lacking Ben's supposed ruthlessness and having nothing to sell that anyone wants to buy, he has come to believe he has to sell himself. If people like him, he incorrectly fantasizes, they will buy from him because of the sheer force of his charismatic personality. This is why Miller never tells us specifically what Willy sells. Having turned himself into a commodity, his products are irrelevant. We can be pretty sure, however, that whatever Willy carries in his bags is just as unappealing as the whipped cheese he eats or the refrigerator that breaks down before he has finished paying for it. Willy's American Dream is little more than a Nightmare Come True of lost sales, cutthroat bosses, cheap cars, snapped fan belts, overdue insurance premiums, late mortgage payments, and an unforgiving son.

When we meet Willy, he's already dead in the sense that his dream of being rich and well liked have made him incapable of dealing with the realities in his life. Not only is he not rich; people don't like him very much. He can't pay his bills, he depends on his neighbor Charley to give him money, and he complains to his wife Linda that he looks foolish and talks too much. Still, he's committed to his dream. So committed, in fact, that he has allowed it to define who he is, and who he is not. The more his sales go down, the harder he pretends he's successful and well liked; the harder he pretends to be successful and well liked, the more he's aware of what a failure he is. This tension between what Willy is and what he's not becomes such a burden you might think he's metaphorically lugging it around in those heavy suitcases he carries at the beginning of the play.

But not many people can carry this kind of psychological baggage without soon becoming mentally exhausted. So what does Willy do to relieve himself of his burden? He fantasizes about a time before the stock market crash of 1929 when the economy was sound, he could make a living in sales, and his sons adored him. On the night we meet him, he was supposed to have driven to Portland, Maine, but he didn't go far beyond his home in Brooklyn before he started dreaming he was in his 1928 Chevy. The windshield was open, he was enjoying the scenery, the warm air was streaming over him, and the next thing he knew he was going off the road. Had he swerved in a different direction, he might have hit something. Or somebody.

Willy's daydreams, however, are not just escapist fantasies. They're psychological projections of what he wants to have in his mind: the time when his boys waxed his car, told him how much they missed him, and vied for his attention. Unfortunately for Willy, his mind doesn't always do everything he wants because it's reeling under the pressure of no longer being able to cope with reality. Events he doesn't want to be reminded of keep intruding, like the time Biff failed math, traveled to Boston, and discovered his father with a woman in a hotel room.

A crisis of this magnitude might pressure some fathers to question their values and change their behavior. Not Willy. He's spent so many years cultivating an image of himself as someone who is both successful and respected, he cannot accept responsibility for what he's done without having to admit he's the phony Biff accuses him of being. It's safer and easier to blame on spite his son's unwillingness to finish high school and his inability to find a well-paying job at the age of thirty-four.

Willy behaves in a similar way when, at the end of the play, Biff confronts him with the idea that they are both a "dime a dozen." He sees through Biff's tears that his son loves him for who he is and forgives him for what he is not, but rather than accept the love he's always wanted and enjoy the relief that will come from no longer having to pretend he's a success, Willy insists on maintaining his false image. He knows that to abandon the myth that he's carried around for all these years would reduce him from a failure to a fool. He'd rather be dead than be seen as the ridiculous person he has become. But Willy's suicide is brought on not only by the fear of finally having to face the truth about himself; his suicide also gives him another opportunity to turn his dream of being successful and well-liked into reality. It's not just the path of least resistance; in his distorted mind, it's the only logical conclusion. Now when he talks in his imagination with Ben, Willy is no longer escaping from an unpleasant situation in the present: he's planning his family's future. Like his role model brother, he can enter unexplored territory and produce wealth with the insurance money that will come from his death. And, like Dave Singleman, he can top off his demise with a funeral attended by hundreds of adoring people.

Willy's dream, however, falls short of its promise. Only four people—his immediate family and his friend Charley—attend his funeral, and if the company that issued his life insurance policy can prove his death is a suicide, Willy's family will not receive the $20,000 he has in mind for them. Without that money, Willy's death—like the life he's imagined for himself—will not have amounted to anything he values.

It didn't have to be this way. At the end of the play when Linda, Biff, Happy, and Charley are standing over Willy's grave, Biff talks about the times when Willy was off the road and working with his hands: building the stoop, finishing the cellar, constructing a new porch, hanging a ceiling, putting up a garage. This is when he was most happy.

Then and when he was enjoying nature. On the evening

when we first meet Willy, he tells his wife how, just before he swerved off the road in Yonkers, he was appreciating the scenery: "It's so beautiful up there, Linda, the trees are so thick and the sun is warm." When he begins to break down after being fired from his job and abandoned by his sons in the restaurant, Willy turns to nature and to working with his hands for comfort. He races to the hardware store for seeds to plant in his backyard even though it is the middle of the night and the ground is too hard to grow anything. The action is also symbolic. Willy runs for seeds because he refuses to surrender his ambition to be successful and admired. But there's little hope in the life he's made for himself, and the ground on which he's trying to produce a future for his family is no longer fertile.

This conflict between Willy's ambition to be financially successful and the satisfaction he experiences when working with his hands in a natural environment is underscored by the stage lighting. Whenever Willy fantasizes about the good times in his life, the lighting emphasizes the trees that used to grow around the Lomans' home. Whenever Willy is upset by the reality he can't escape, the lighting focuses on the apartment buildings that have replaced the trees and prevent the sun from shining on the Lomans' property. Biff says it best when he tells the mourners at Willy's grave: "There's more of him in that front stoop than all the sales he ever made." In other words, Willy should have supported himself and his family doing what he enjoyed most: working with his hands. He might not have become rich, but he and his family would have had a better chance of being happy.

Where did Willy go wrong? Probably when, as a child, he began admiring his absent father. Most of what he knows about this man is from stories told to him by his brother. We learn that the father lives in Willy's imagination as an accomplished musician, and successful pioneer. He'd put his family in a wagon and traveled all over the country selling the flutes he carved along the way. Somewhere along the way of this story, however, Willy missed an important point: his father made money by doing what he liked most and what he did best. Had Willy followed the model set for him in his imagination by his father, he might have increased his chances for success and affection. Did you notice how the sound of a flute permeates so many scenes in the play? Think how it must haunt Willy's imagination.

What Ben doesn't tell Willy, and probably doesn't know, is why their father left his young wife and their two children. When the seventeen-year-old Ben also leaves the family to make his fortune, he's following in his father's footsteps. But Willy can't follow in theirs. He doesn't have the same sense of independence or the ambition to do what they did. He's too insecure. He's too concerned with acquiring the love he believes he never received from his father and the approval he always seems to want from Ben. His sons are the same way. Happy is forever trying to please his father with promises to lose weight, make money, and get married, but Willy barely notices him because his attention is continually focused on the older, favored Biff. And whereas Biff can light out for unknown territory, learn to appreciate life on the range, and see where he went wrong from the view provided him by a prison cell, he too needs to feel that his father loves him. This is one of the reasons that he keeps returning home. Having discovered Willy with a woman in a hotel room, he fears that his father's love for his family is phony. But unlike Happy, who tries to earn Willy's love by doing what he thinks his father will approve of, Biff challenges his father to love him in spite of the fact that he is a bum and a thief.

Because Willy has failed to strike out on his own and make money, he has failed in his mind to become a man. But instead of examining his condition and coming to an understanding of who he is as a person, he covers up with lies the distance separating his real self from the image he wants everyone to have of him. The false number of sales he makes, the exaggerated warmth of the receptions he receives, and the ludicrous number of friends he says he has are all designed to hide from himself and others the fundamental truth that he is emotionally still a boy. Not surprisingly, Willy's tactics work only on himself and his immature sons.

Willy uses his sons to make him look good. But because they reflect the false values of success and admiration their father has projected onto them, they will never be able to make him look as he wants to appear. Like their father, they remain immature and dishonest boys: Happy is sexually competitive with his bosses, and Biff steals everything from footballs to fountain pens.

Wanting to be rich, needing to be well liked, confusing money with manhood, mistaking dreams for reality, failing to examine the commercial values that define his life, and choosing the ultimate form of escape as a solution to his problems, Willy has been deemed unworthy of genuine heroic stature by many critics. They claim he is nothing more than a pathetic loser. Three critics in a single article tell us, "Willy's self-destruction . . . is the despairing ill-considered act of immaturity. If we reject Willy, it is because he is only potentially a hero." William Beyer concurs that, Willy is "too petty, commonplace, and immature" to be a hero. Miller—as you might expect—disagrees. "Willy is a very brave spirit who cannot settle for half but must pursue his dream of himself to the end." What's your opinion? Is Willy's suicide an opportunity to finally escape from the reality that is so quickly closing in on him, or is it the ultimate sign of love? In his mind, isn't he laying down his life so his family can be financially secure? If he had stepped in front of a bus to prevent Linda from being run over, we would say he's heroic. Why can't we say the same in the case of this suicide? What's the difference? Is it possible to see Willy's death as a triumph over the

On Ideals

The trouble with Willy Loman is that he has tremendously powerful ideals. . . . If Willy Loman, for instance, had not had a very profound sense that his life as lived had left him hollow, he would have died contentedly polishing his car on some Sunday afternoon at a ripe old age. The fact is that he has values. The fact that they cannot be realized is what is driving him mad, just as, unfortunately, it is driving a lot of other people mad. The truly valueless man, the man without ideals, is always perfectly at home anywhere because there cannot be conflict between nothing and something.

—Arthur Miller

circumstances that have limited him, or has he just finally caved in to the pressure brought upon him by circumstances of his own making? Does his ultimate sacrifice allow him to transcend the mediocre condition of his life and achieve the dignity many of the play's critics say he lacks, or does his suicide by its very nature relegate him to the realm of the cowardly and irresponsible? Could the experts who see Willy as a pathetic character rather than a heroic one be missing something? Or is Miller trying to make too much of his little salesman?

Whether we see Willy as heroic or pathetic, we can't help but feel sorry for him. Charley tells us that "Nobody dast blame this man." How could we? Who among us hasn't been influenced by the commercial forces that corrupt Willy? Or hasn't rationalized failure? Or mistaken illusions for ideals? Or wanted to be rich and loved? Or been true to himself or herself and others? Is it wrong for Willy to want his family to be financially secure? Is he less of a person because he seeks a place of respect in his sons' memories? At least he didn't wind up insensitive like his boss Howard. Nor did he give up his dream and look for comfort in the trash heap of commodities that have outlived their usefulness. In a world where all do not succeed and there is little room for hope, Willy refuses to be passive. He continues to fight against all challenges to his dignity.

Linda Loman

If Miller intended us to see this play from the inside of Willy's head, we might also consider looking at it from the viewpoint of his wife Linda's heart. Warm, sympathetic, caring, and encouraging, she's probably the main reason why the three other Lomans are still talking to each other. She tolerates Happy's indifference to his family, makes excuses for Biff's inability to settle down, and sticks with Willy in spite of the often abusive ways he treats her. Biff and Happy can talk with Linda about subjects they can't discuss with their father, and Linda is the only person with whom Willy can be honest up to a point. He does not tell her about his affair in Boston of course. In fact, he is able to confess to Linda what he has a hard time admitting to himself: people laugh at him, pass him by, and say he talks too much. He doesn't dress to his advantage and is short, fat, and looks foolish. Linda responds by lovingly telling him that he's wonderful, successful, lively, handsome, and idolized by his sons.

Linda takes care of Willy and is fiercely loyal to him. She makes sure all the bills are paid before they are past due, saves money by mending her stockings rather than buying new ones, and when their sons are critical of him, defends Willy as "the dearest man in the world." She won't accept Happy's excuses for abandoning his father in a restaurant, refuses to allow Biff to torment Willy with the reasons why they are both failures, and even goes so far as to order her sons to leave their house, live in Happy's apartment, and not return.

If only Linda could speak to Willy the way she speaks to Biff and Happy! She never shrinks from pointing out their failings to them—calling one a "bum," the other a "louse," and both "a pair of animals"— but she always falls short of confronting her husband with his. If Willy can for the most part be honest with her, why can't she be a little more straightforward with him? Perhaps this is one of her ways of making their marriage work. Perhaps she knows how badly he depends on her to support his fragile ego. Perhaps she fears that Willy wouldn't be able to take criticism from someone less submissive. Perhaps she's right. Perhaps like many traditional wives who've bought into the image of the successful homemaker, she's learned from experience what she needs to do to survive.

Remember when Biff and Happy are discussing their plans to go into business together, and every time Linda wants to say something, Willy tells her to stop interrupting? No sooner does Biff tell his father to stop being disrespectful than Linda is on her son's case for lessening Willy's enthusiasm for their absurd business venture. Is it possible that Linda long ago chose to be Willy's doormat because she doesn't want to jeopardize her own financial security by raising issues she fears would lead to arguments or perhaps even a divorce? And what would Linda do if Willy decided to replace her with someone more compliant? How does a woman with little education, few marketable skills, and no work experience survive in a world like the one the Loman men inhabit?

In the 1940s, few women were able to work outside the home. Whatever the reason for her reticence, Linda's support, tolerance, and protection haven't helped her husband very much. She may, in fact, have done more harm than good by enabling him to remain immature. Isn't Willy racing to his death with dreams of Biff booting a football the same person who encouraged his favored son to steal building materials, cheat at math, and be well liked by his peers? How has he changed? Stealing from his insurance company and cheating his family of his presence in order to be loved, Willy is still a poster child for taking the "fun" out of "dysfunctional."

By offering encouragement rather than understanding and by supporting illusions rather than truths—think of her decision not to remove the rubber hose from the gas heater because she doesn't want to "insult" Willy—Linda has contributed to the tragedy that engulfs the Loman family long before her husband even thinks of killing himself. How did she do this? By believing in a myth that's just as powerful and false as the one Willy has sacrificed his life for: that of the good woman who stands behind every successful man. By keeping her mouth shut, maintaining a tidy house, making sure the family's finances are in order, and raising their children, Linda expects as her due to be taken care of in return.

And how does Willy show his appreciation for the sacrifices his wife has made? He has treated her, according to Biff, without an ounce of respect, failed to provide her with the financial security she has earned by keeping the family together for more than thirty-five years, and cheated on her with one woman who is every bit as coarse, self-centered, and opportunistic as he is. While Willy provides the woman in Boston with new silk stockings and receives greater access to her employer's buyers in return, his wife mends her old stockings in Brooklyn and is treated shabbily in return. Linda's image of Willy as a loyal husband is almost as distorted as his images are of everyone else. No wonder she can't understand why he killed himself. "Why did you ever do that?" she asks him as she stands over his grave. "I search and search and I search, and I can't understand it, Willy. I made the final payment on the house today. Today, dear. And there'll be nobody home."

The Loman Brothers

Make no mistake about it: Biff and Happy are their father's sons. He has taught them to want to be rich and well liked and to equate success with what it means to be a man. They've played violent sports without learning much about sportsmanship; are competitive but not above playing unfairly; don't show much respect for women other than their mother; and like their father, are trapped in an adolescent stage of development that contributes to their profound senses of inferiority.

Happy is the less attractive of the two brothers because he's most like his father. Loud and dull, he wants to be the No. 1 Man in his company, but, like Willy, lacks Uncle Ben's daring and Dave Singleman's charm. So he sets his myopic sights on nothing more challenging than inheriting the job of the merchandise manager, who will have to die before this Low-Man can be promoted. Until that day comes, Happy satisfies his thirst for adventure and what he calls his "overdeveloped sense of competition" by engaging in such high-minded activities as accepting kickbacks from vendors, taking off time from work at his company's expense, and seducing the fiancées of three of his bosses.

Happy also falls short of being No. 1 in the Well-Liked Department because he has always come in No. 2 to his older brother. Biff is the one who gets all the praise and most of the attention. Biff is the gridiron hero for whom the University of Virginia has a special interest; the heartthrob for whom the girls pay when he goes on dates; the hero for whom the boys clean out the Lomans' furnace; the idol for whom his neighbor Bernard provides the answers on math tests; the star on whom Willy places his highest hopes; and the savior to whom Linda turns for help in solving her husband's plight. Happy is not nearly as fortunate. Neither of his parents pay much attention to him unless he seeks it, and their response is always less than he'd hoped. Whenever he asks his father to notice the weight he's lost, Willy doesn't so much as glance his way, and when he tells his mother he's going to get married, Linda tells him to get some sleep.

Happy has an opportunity to contribute in a significant way to his family's well-being and gain some longed-for recognition after Biff returns home and Linda reveals the circumstances that are leading Willy to think about killing himself. His response? A crackpot adolescent scheme that includes athletic competition, economic success, and social advancement. Biff and Happy, the Loman Brothers, will sell sporting goods by giving exhibitions. They'll travel the country just like their famous grandfather. Basketball, boxing, whatever. It'll be like high school all over again. And who's going to come up with the $10,000 stake they need to get started? None other than Bill Oliver, the successful entrepreneur for whom Biff once worked as a shipping clerk and from whom he stole merchandise.

What Happy lacks between his ears he compensates for with what's between his legs. We see him do this while waiting in the restaurant for Biff and his father. Admiring the "binoculars" on a "piece of strudel," he hits on a woman who isn't much different in appearance and attitude from the one his father had an affair with in Boston. The lies Happy tells the woman would be laughable if they weren't so sad: he sells champagne, he attended West Point, and his brother is a quarterback for the New York Giants. He then sends the woman out to find a friend for Biff. By the time she returns, we've learned that Biff never got to see Bill Oliver, and the boys have discovered Willy has been fired from his job. These setbacks drive Willy into the men's room to wrestle with his worst nightmare—the day Biff discovered him cheating on Linda—and Biff runs from the restaurant in frustration over his brother's being more concerned with the women he has picked up than their dad. Happy suggests that he and the women follow Biff, but when one of them wants to tell his father that they're leaving, whatever sympathy we might have had for the younger brother starts heading in the opposite direction: "That's not my father," he tells the woman. "He's just a guy."

Of course, Happy doesn't see himself as unsympathetic. In his mind, he's the loyal son who looks after his parents while the favored son searches for himself on a ranch; treats Willy and Linda to a vacation in Florida; remains optimistic about and loyal to the family's dream of being successful; and fights to be No. 1 so his father will not have lived in vain. In return he asks only for the freedom to have an apartment of his own and to spend a disproportionate share of his income on women. Had his family cared more about him, do you think Happy might have grown up to be more sensitive, as Biff? Or do you think because of the values Willy instilled in him, Happy has been programmed from an early age never to be more than a shadow of his failed brother and a parody of his pathetic father? It's hard to say, but there is little doubt that the role he has been cast to play in his family structure has had an adverse affect on his development as a human being.

Like Happy, Biff was taught from an early age his father's lessons about the hard work and perseverance it takes to be successful, well liked, and manly. "The world is an oyster, but you don't crack it open on a mattress," Willy told his boys. "Never leave a job till you're finished." And he practiced what he preached. He may never have made all the sales he claimed, but Willy did manage to pay his bills within their grace periods, Linda never had to work, and occasionally he was able to head home with enough extra money to pick up presents for his boys along the way.

Biff followed his father's words and the role models he wanted them to imitate: he spared no elbow grease on the family car and had to have worked hard to become the quarterback on his football team. With success came the adulation he was told would follow. And the behavior he could get away with. His father didn't think it odd when Linda complained that Biff was a little too rough with the girls he dated, and Biff didn't think having his friends complete his chores around the house while he tossed the pigskin with Happy in the backyard was in any way extraordinary. This was all part of what it meant to be a star. When Biff stole a football from his coach despite Happy's warning that their dad would disapprove, Willy praised the boy for his "initiative." Initiative led Biff to steal building supplies from a local construction site, and he accepted as his due the answers Bernard gave him on math exams.

But Bernard couldn't give Biff enough answers to prevent him from failing math in his senior year. Panicked that his college football scholarships might be in jeopardy, Biff impulsively rushed to Boston to ask his father to talk the math teacher into giving him the four points he needed to graduate. When he arrived unexpectedly, he discovered Willy with a woman in his hotel room.

This betrayal hit Biff harder than anything he ever experienced on a football field. He concluded that his father was a phony, and so were the values he preached. Choosing not to make up his failing grade in summer school, nor attend college in the fall, and not to embark on a career of subways, sales, and two-week annual vacations, Biff headed west to earn his living with his hands. Why do you think he behaved this way? Why sacrifice his future just because his father failed to live up to the image he'd created in the family's collective mind?

Because Biff isn't able to resolve the issues arising from his father's infidelity, he is still immature when he returns to Brooklyn at the age of thirty-four after again failing to find himself at home on the range. "I'm not married, I'm not in business," he tells Happy. "I'm like a boy." What Biff doesn't realize is that no matter how far from Brooklyn he may roam, he's still emotionally dependent on his father. He is still a boy. The difference between now and when he was a kid, however, is that whereas Biff once sought Willy's approval by acting the way his father wanted him to, he now seeks his father's love by being the person he thinks he has become: someone who's not willing to play Willy's phony games of loyalty and success. Biff, like a rebellious teenager, wants his father to approve of this son. He doesn't realize that for Willy to respond positively he would have to admit he failed to live up to the values with which he brainwashed his children. In fact, the more Willy's economic condition worsens, the more desperate are his attempts to convince himself that, if he's not exactly as successful, well liked, and manly as he had hoped he would be at the age of sixty-three, at least he was successful, well liked, and manly in the past as he imagines it.

Willy isn't the only Loman who creates a false image to protect himself from the truth of who he is. Biff does it too. He may be determined to show his father he can be his own kind of man his own kind of way, but he can't do better than drift aimlessly from job to job because he continues to repeat the acts of petty thievery his father once applauded as initiative. Biff may look like a man, but he's still the boy who looked for praise by acting in ways his father approved. And the longer he goes without winning his father's acceptance, the more desperate and counterproductive his behavior becomes. It's one thing to "borrow" a football from your coach without asking; it's quite another to wind up in jail on a conviction for larceny. What do you think Biff unknowingly feels has been stolen from him that he has to steal back in the form of a football or a two-by-four or a fountain pen? When Biff doesn't write to his parents for three months because he doesn't want them to know his address is a prison, he's ashamed of the behavior that led to his conviction, but he's also unconsciously sending his father other messages by his silence:

Have you noticed you haven't heard from me? Whose fault is that? And if you knew where I was, would you still love me? Because I already know the answers, I'm going to make you suffer by having Mom worry about me.

Absence may be one of the greatest forms of presence, but it isn't a solution. As long as Biff steals, he guarantees his failure to succeed on his own terms. And the more he fails, the more he convinces his father he's acting out of spite. In Willy's mind, Biff refuses to forgive him for seeking a little affection to ease his loneliness. In Biff's mind, his father's reasoning is a poor excuse for acting in a way that is inconsistent with the values he taught his sons. The sad truth is that Willy's behavior is entirely consistent with his values. His taking the initiative to cheat on Linda isn't much different from encouraging his sons to cheat in school, steal from construction sites, and take advantage of whatever other opportunities might arise. Biff is right in a way he's unaware of when he says there's more of Willy in the family's front stoop than in all the sales Willy ever made. That stoop, like the lives of Willy and his sons, is built out of materials that haven't been earned. In a symbolic sense, they are phony because they represent the false foundation upon which the Lomans' whole value system has been built. What Biff doesn't realize about all this is that he's using Willy's false values as an excuse to avoid looking for the real causes of his own failure, namely, his inability to live without his father's approval.

Isn't it amazing how the more different Biff thinks he is from his father the more he resembles him? Hasn't Willy also wasted much of his life behaving in ways that would endear him to the father he never knew and his surrogate father, Ben? The difference between Biff and Willy, of course, is that Biff acquires the self-knowledge he needs to grow up; this is the same self-knowledge his father kills himself to avoid. Here's how Biff does it: remember when he went to see Bill Oliver to ask him to finance the Loman brothers' new sporting goods company? And remember when Biff becomes so frustrated at having to wait all day that he steals the pen from Oliver's desk? That pen, which some psychologists say is a phallic representation of manhood, symbolizes the significance of Biff's realization that he wasn't a salesman for Oliver. He was only a shipping clerk. There's no way Oliver would stake the Loman brothers' company. Especially if he remembered that Biff was the same guy who stole athletic equipment.

By the time he reaches the restaurant where he and Happy plan to treat Willy to dinner, Biff has changed from a boy who was willing to cooperate in another lie about his past to a man who is willing to accept the truth that he's no longer the wonderful talent his father cracked him up to be. He may have been a star on the gridiron in high school, but today he's just a plain, ordinary human being.

Rather than be depressed by the realization that he's a "dime-a-dozen," however, Biff is relieved. He no longer has to pretend he's someone he's not. Now he can work with his hands on a ranch under an open sky without feeling guilty because he doesn't have his father's approval. But because he loves his father and his brother and wants them to be happy, he doesn't want to leave Brooklyn without telling them about his discovery. If they can let go of the false values that have imprisoned them all their lives, they too can be who they are.

The problem for Happy and Willy, of course, is that they, like Biff, are nobodies, but, unlike Biff, this is not a truth they can accept. In fact, it makes them even more determined to succeed where they think Biff has failed. As a result, Willy winds up killing himself in a stupid, unnecessary, and most likely flawed attempt to earn the insurance money he imagines will secure his family's financial future. Happy, on the other hand, mistakenly sees Biff's decision to go his own way as a betrayal of their father's dream. "Willy Loman did not die in vain," he tells his brother. "He fought it out here, and this is where I'm gonna win it for him." Poor Happy. He's as misdirected as his dad. And what about Biff? What name would you use to describe him? "Lucky" because he no longer has to go through life trying to be someone he's not? "Free" because he no longer has to feel guilty about not following his father's example? "Rich" because what he learned about himself is of greater value than any material success? "Mature" because he's finally accepted responsibility for his behavior and grown in ways his father and brother avoided? Can you think of others?

Charley, Bernard, and Howard

Charley, Bernard, and Howard are what writers call "reflector" characters. Never central to the play, almost always one-dimensional, they rarely change their thinking or behavior. Their job from the playwright's point of view is to reflect in some way on the issues the main characters are trying to come to terms with. As reflector characters, Charley and Howard provide two different images of the capitalist system from which Willy learns the importance of being successful.

For Willy's boss Howard, sales are what count. Anyone who can't turn a profit is of no value. He doesn't care if Willy has worked for his company when it belonged to his father. How much money this Loman has made for Howard and his family over the past thirty-four years is also history. You can't deposit the past in a bank account. And Willy, who can no longer sell enough merchandise to pay his own bills, doesn't hold much promise for future profits. He may think he opened the New England territory, and even if he did, he now falls asleep at the wheel of his car and can't keep all of his appointments. In fact, Willy's sales have been so low, Howard has taken him off his supplemental salary and put him on a strict commission. When Willy says he doesn't want to travel anymore, Howard tells him "business is business." When Willy asks him for a position in the New York department store, Howard says he doesn't have any room for someone who "can't pull his own weight." When Willy says he only needs a job that will pay forty dollars a week, Howard tells him he "can't get blood from a stone." Then, when Willy resigns himself to his miserable life on the road, Howard fires him. Nothing personal. Just business as business. And Howard's final words to the man who's devoted most of his life to making him rich? "Don't forget to return the samples."

Charley is the kinder, gentler face of capitalism. Successful and compassionate, he has made the compromises needed to earn money, but he hasn't given up his genuine concern for the welfare of others. He's the only real friend Willy has and the only person besides Linda to understand the seriousness of his condition. This is why, when Willy is upset that Biff may return to Texas on another wild goose chase to find himself, the clear-thinking, hard-headed businessman advises his friend to let him go: "When the deposit bottle is broken, you don't get your nickel back." It's not that Charley doesn't care about Biff. He does. But he also knows when and how much to care. After Howard puts Willy on commission, Charley gives his friend fifty dollars a week to supplement his income and offers him a job to maintain his dignity.

In the same way that Howard and Charley juxtapose one another, so too do Biff and Charley's son Bernard. Whereas Biff is a hero, Bernard is a nerd. He wears thick glasses, dresses in geek clothes, does all his homework, and provides Biff with the answers he needs to pass his exams in school. Willy refers to him as "anemic," and Biff tells his dad Bernard is liked, but he's not the all-important "well-liked." If Bernard feels diminished by or harbors any resentment over the treatment he receives at the hands of the Lomans, he doesn't show it. At least not when he's grown up. While Biff is sitting broke and confused in the childhood bedroom he once shared with Happy, Bernard is preparing to argue a case in front of the Supreme Court.

So how did Charley and Bernard get to be so good? How did they manage to stay above the ambition, selfishness, and greed that seduces just about everybody else? Even when they're bad—Bernard helping Biff cheat in math and Charley helping Willy deceive Linda with fifty dollar handouts—they're good. Charley says his secret is that he "never took any interest in anything." What does he mean by that? Does it seem too simple an answer? Why do you think Miller shows Charley's and Bernard's good behavior without giving us an explanation for it? And why do you think Willy is so blind to what's so obvious to us?

Chapter 3

Narrative Strategies

MILLER USES SO MANY TECHNIQUES to move his story and convey the meanings of his play that they're almost as important as his characters. The flute music that haunts Willy is like a never-ending, ever-repeating theme that contrasts his dream of success with the reality of his circumstances. Lighting alters with the flick of a switch our mood as well as our perspective as we witness action within either a pastoral or an urban setting. The stage set with its roof open to either a heaven of trees or a hell of apartment buildings and the imagined walls of the Lomans' home can take us in into the past and back to the present in seconds. Not only does this skeletal set make our journey into Willy's imagination more believable, we don't have to sit waiting in the dark for props to be moved whenever the scene changes. Free from having to worry about maintaining our attention through the pauses that would occur on a more realistic set, Miller moves his characters through time and space with a minimum of props. And instead of having to create a narrator or have his characters fill us in on the Lomans' history, he makes the past an integral part of the action.

This technique of having the past that takes place in Willy's imagination appear as real as any behavior being acted out in present time on the stage comes mostly from a dramatic tradition known as "Expressionism." Expressionist writers such as the Norwegian playwright Henrik Ibsen—a major influence on Miller's work—believe that the past, the imagination, and the unconscious are as real as any action we can see, and should be expressed on stage in equally real terms. The past, the imagination, and the unconscious in the minds of these writers not only inform the present, they *are* the present. By combining Willy's past with his present in the real time of the action taking place on the stage, Miller can have two plots running almost simultaneously: the "exterior" plot of the last day in Willy's life, and the "interior" plot that runs from Willy's earliest memories of Biff playing football to the memory he'd most like to forget: the day his son discovered him cheating on Linda.

The specific way Miller forges Willy's past with his present into one continuous action is through flashbacks. Whenever something occurs in the present that makes Willy uncomfortable, he tries to escape into a pleasant time in his past. But Willy's memories, which are dramatized by the characters in the play, often seem to have minds of their own. Some of these memories contain a kind of emotional charge that creates for Willy even more tension in his present. And this emotional charge is often so strong Willy has a hard time separating his past from his present. In fact, his past becomes his present. The most powerful example of how this works occurs in the climactic restaurant scene when Biff is trying to tell Willy he didn't get to ask Bill Oliver to stake the brothers' sporting goods company. Willy can sense the direction their conversation is headed, and in an attempt to protect himself from the pain of disappointment, drifts into his memory bank. But what awaits him is not Biff polishing the car or scoring a winning touchdown. He has to once again live through the day Bernard informed him of Biff's flunking math. While Bernard (in the "past") tells Willy Biff won't be able to graduate, Willy (in the "present") tries to tell Biff that if he hadn't flunked math he would have made something of himself. Biff, of course, doesn't know what his father is talking about. What does flunking math have to do with seeing Oliver? This technique of having Willy simultaneously talk to Bernard in the

past and Biff in the present? It is called "stichomythic dia-
logue." "Stichomythic" comes from a Greek word meaning
"to speak in alternating lines."

When Happy reveals that Biff stole Oliver's pen, Willy,
who's already reeling from being fired earlier in the afternoon, has about all he can take of the present. But he can't
find any solace in the past as his mind flashes on the day
Biff discovered him with a woman in his hotel room. Biff
can see his father is having a breakdown, but all Happy
can think about is the two women he's picked up.
Frustrated by his brother's lack of concern for their father
and shocked by the extent of Willy's breakdown, Biff runs
from the restaurant. Happy and the women follow, and
Willy is left abandoned in a men's room to face the music
of Biff's reaction to his infidelity. When he comes out of
the latest rerun of his nightmare from hell, Willy discovers
Biff and Happy have left without paying the bill.

Tragedy or Soap Opera?

A little more than 2,300 years ago, Aristotle sat down and
came up with a list of criteria that could determine when
a play could be considered a tragedy. One criterion is that
the hero of the play has to be a highly respected human
being: a king, a general, the captain of a ship, a person
with that kind of stature. But this kind of protagonist
must also have a tragic flaw, a failing that leads to a
downfall that another hero might have been able to avoid.
Pride is the most common flaw of tragic heroes, but there
are others: jealousy, ambition, lust, inability to make a
decision, fear of taking action. The list is as long as there
are human failings. And because the tragic hero is held in
such high esteem, his or her fall is a big one. Most tragic
heroes wind up dead. But their horrible ends, according to
Aristotle, shouldn't make us just sad or depressed. They
should also inspire what he calls a "catharsis." What he

means by this is that in the same way tragic heroes come to recognize and understand the flaws that led to their downfalls, so too should we be able to recognize, understand, and purge ourselves of similar flaws in our own characters.

Since *Death of a Salesman* opened in 1949, academics have been debating whether the play is a tragedy or just a sad story about a family of losers. Those who take the latter point of view claim that Willy is not a respected representative of humankind. As his name indicates, he's a Low-man. Although he has plenty of flaws, he doesn't suffer a great downfall because he's already among society's cellar dwellers, morally as well as physically. Rather than fight against the forces working against him, he caves in to them. What kind of hero is that? He doesn't even understand why he wants to kill himself. And as for a catharsis, these academics are willing to concede that Willy's experience has something to teach us about the danger of holding on too tightly to false values, but that's not enough to deem the play worthy of Aristotle's definition. Willy Loman isn't tragic; he's pathetic.

Miller thinks this debate is pointless academic quibbling. To begin with, it's unfair to measure his play against standards created more than two thousand years ago. As Miller points out in his "Introduction to the *Collected Plays*," Aristotle never had to pay off a mortgage. Miller also claims the academics who don't think Willy Loman has suffered a great fall have confused stature with rank. What does it matter if Willy is a salesman or a nobleman as long as he's committed to a respectable course of action? And how many greater acts of love are there than that of a father willing to lay down his life for his family? Willy is not depressed or resigned as he rushes to his death; he's exultant knowing that Biff loves him. Talk

On Success

I always said that New England territory was no damn good.

—Anonymous Theatergoer

Unlike the law against incest, the law of success is not administered by statute or church, but it is very nearly as powerful in its grip upon man. The confusion increases because, while it is a law, it is by no means a wholly agreeable one even as it is slavishly obeyed, for to fail is no longer to belong to society. . . . Therefore, the path is opened for those who wish to call Willy merely a foolish man even as they themselves are living in obedience to the same law that killed him.

—Arthur Miller

about a catharsis! He's finally achieved the fatherhood for which he has striven to reclaim since his disastrous indiscretion in the Boston hotel room. In pursuing the respect he wants his family to have for him, Willy—in his mind—is a hero.

What do you think? Is Miller naive or overly sentimental in thinking weak, deluded, childish Willy is a hero? Or is Willy's dogged determination to be successful and well-liked admirable? Is he, as Biff says during the restaurant scene, a "prince," or is he, as Happy says in the same scene, "just a guy"?

Debating the question: Tragedy or Melodrama?

Willy is not a tragic figure. For whatever else a tragic figure may be, he is one who has come to know himself.
—Joseph Hynes

Plain souls like this salesman are of interest to their families and to God; but we need greatness to inspire us.
—Judah Bierman, James Hart, and Stanley Johnson

The play, with its peculiar hodgepodge of dated material and facile new ones, is not tragedy at all but an ambitious piece of confusionism, such as in any other sphere would probably be called a hoax, and which has been put across by purely technical skills not unlike those of a magician or acrobat.
—Eleanor Clark

When the literary critics measure the play against Greek and Elizabethan drama, they agree . . . the hero seems inadequate. His lack of stature, his narrow view of reality, his obvious character defects diminish the scope of action and the possibilities of human application. Against a large historical perspective and without the American context, the salesman is a "small man" who fails to cope with his environment.
—Thomas Porter

The play was always heroic to me, and in later years the academy's charge that Willy lacked "stature" for the tragic hero seemed incredible to me. I had not understood that these matters are measured by Greco-Elizabethan paragraphs which hold no mention of insurance payments, front porches, refrigerator fan belts . . .
—Arthur Miller

Mr. Miller's play is a tragedy modern and personal, not classic and heroic. It's central figure is a little man sentenced to discover his smallness rather than a big man undone by greatness.

—John Mason Brown

I believe that the common man is as apt a subject for tragedy as kings were.

—Arthur Miller

Death of a Salesman is a play written along the lines of the finest classical tragedy. It is the revelation of a man's downfall in destruction whose roots are entirely in his own soul.

—William Hawkins

To me the tragedy of Willy Loman is that he gave his life, or sold it, in order to justify the waste of it. It is the tragedy of a man who did believe that he alone was not meeting the qualifications laid down for mankind by those clean-shaven frontiersmen who inhabit the peaks of broadcasting and advertising offices. From those forests of canned goods high up near the sky, he heard the thundering command to succeed as it ricocheted down the newspaper-lined canyons of his city, heard not a human voice, but a wind of a voice to which no human can reply in kind, except to stare into the mirror at a failure.

—Arthur Miller

thirty-four years into this firm, Howard, and now I can't
a man is not a piece of fruit! I'm talking about your fath
ou've got people to see—I put thirty-four years into this
range and throw the peel away—a man is not a piece of f
his desk! You mustn't tell me you've got people to see—I
y insurance! You can't eat the orange and throw the peel
here were promises made across this desk! You mustn't tel
oward, and now I can't pay my insurance! You can't eat th
alking about your father! There were promises made acros
y-four years into this firm, Howard, and now I can't pay
an is not a piece of fruit! I'm talking about your fathe
ou've got people to see—I put thirty-four years into this
range and throw the peel away—a man is not a piece of f
his desk! You mustn't tell me you've got people to see—I
y insurance! You can't eat the orange and throw the peel
here were promises made across this desk! You mustn't tel
oward, and now I can't pay my insurance! You can't eat th
alking about your father! There were promises made acros
y-four years into this firm, Howard, and now I can't pay
an is not a piece of fruit! I'm talking about your fathe
ou've got people to see—I put thirty-four years into this
range and throw the peel away—a man is not a piece of f
his desk! You mustn't tell me you've got people to see—I
y insurance! You can't eat the orange and throw the peel
here were promises made across this desk! You mustn't tel
oward, and now I can't pay my insurance! You can't eat th
alking about your father! There were promises made acros
y-four years into this firm, Howard, and now I can't pay
an is not a piece of fruit! I'm talking about your fathe
ou've got people to see—I put thirty-four years into this
range and throw the peel away—a man is not a piece of f
his desk! You mustn't tell me you've got people to see—I
y insurance! You can't eat the orange and throw the peel
here were promises made across this desk! You mustn't tel
oward, and now I can't pay my insurance! You can't eat th
alking about your father! There were promises made acros

Part III:
The Crucible

THIS 1855 PAINTING DEPICTS THE TRIAL FOR WITCHCRAFT OF GEORGE JACOBS IN 1692. *THE CRUCIBLE* WAS INSPIRED BY THE NEW ENGLAND WITCHCRAFT TRIALS AS WELL AS THE ANTI-COMMUNIST WITCH HUNT TO WHICH MILLER WAS PREY IN THE 1950s.

Chapter 1

*The Crucible—*Setting the Scene

> How may I live without my name? I have
> given you my soul; leave me my name!
> > John Proctor

THE FIRST PURITANS TO LAND IN 1624 on the shores of
what would one day become the United States of America
were fleeing religious persecution in England. But they
weren't just fleeing from; they were also running toward.
They were searching for a New World where they could
live in peace and follow God's word as they interpreted it
from the Bible. The Puritans named their newfound land
"Massachusetts" after the Massasoit natives who lived
there, but there wasn't much peace or time for reading the
Bible. At least not after the Puritans started treating the
Massasoits in ways similar to those the Puritans had experienced in England.

The Puritans, like many persecuted people who
become persecutors themselves once they gain some power,
created a form of government that was based not on the
democratic principles that failed to protect them in
England but on a restrictive set of directives determined by
the Bible. This kind of government, which considers faith
to be a more reliable guide for acceptable behavior than
reason, is called a "theocracy." As more and more Puritans
arrived in Massachusetts, more and more Massasoits got
pushed from wherever the Puritans wanted to settle. By
1626, the Puritans had founded the town of Salem on the
shores north of Boston. "Salem" comes from the Hebrew
word "Shalom," meaning "peace." Given the way they'd

been treating the Massasoits and the way the Massasoits had been responding, "Salem" was probably more a dream than a reality, but the Pilgrims were determined to have their peace.

How far the Puritans would go to get their way became apparent when they hanged nineteen of their own people and two dogs in 1692. While the last colonist was being strung up on the town gallows, fifty men and women waited for their turn in the noose and one hundred and fifty others were slated to stand trial. All for the sin of witchcraft. A sin so terrible there was only one way—according to the Bible—to eliminate it in those who refused to confess, repent, and change their behavior: death.

But what was witchcraft? The Puritans didn't exactly know. They believed that witches did the devil's work on Earth the same way Christian ministers labored on God's behalf. Witches were said to communicate with the devil through birds and small animals known as "familiars"—this explains the deaths of the two dogs—and they could "send out their spirits" to cause trouble in the lives of others. Witches recruited people to the devil's side by appearing to them in dreams or visions and were invisible to all but their victims. What the victims saw when under the influence of witches or the devil was called "spectral shapes."

In addition to those hanged, one man was pressed to death by rocks for refusing to cooperate. All of the accusers were females between the ages of nine and twenty. Their testimony was often accompanied by fainting and the hysterical fits they could whip themselves into when naming the people they claimed were witches. Because many of the accusers were children and considered by the Puritans to be too young to have chosen to be contaminated by sin, the only possible explanation for their behavior was that they had been possessed by the devil. And the devil, as every Salemite knew, was working day and night with the heathen Massasoits to overthrow the Puritan community and stop Christianity from spreading in the New World.

When one-fourth of all those accused of witchcraft not only confessed but were somehow able to provide substantial details of their conspiracies with the devil, mass hysteria broke out. The Puritans thought their community had been undermined from within. Its people were its own worst enemy. Nobody could be trusted. And the knowledge that Satan had been an angel of God before he turned bad also meant that nobody was safe. Anyone, no matter how respectable, could be denounced on unreliable "spectral" evidence that was difficult if not impossible to disprove.

People who held grudges saw those they begrudged as witches. People who wanted to own other people's lands saw the owners as witches. People who held differing political views saw each other as witches. People who owed money were witches. People who demanded they be paid were witches. In the spring of 1692, there were more witches in Salem than there were horse flies. And the witches were regenerating at a faster pace. All the witches quickly disappeared, however, when church leaders in Boston decided that "spectral" evidence wasn't enough to warrant hanging someone. Shortly afterward, the Massachusetts theocracy also vanished.

Flash-forward to February of 1950. You're in Wheeling, West Virginia. You're listening to Wisconsin Senator Joseph P. McCarthy deliver a speech to the Ohio County Women's Republican Club. McCarthy's face is red. He is shouting in anger and waving some papers. These papers, he claims, list the names of more than two hundred communists who are right now as he speaks working like the devil to overthrow the American government through their jobs at the State Department.

McCarthy and other government leaders are coordinating their efforts with those in business, education, and industry to create a climate of fear that will help sustain the powerful economy created in the United States during World War II. They believe that without a war a lot of businesses will have to close. People will lose their jobs, and the country will be in danger of slipping into an economic depression. To keep employment high and make sure the rich who got richer from the war will get even richer from the peace, government leaders are representing America as a military target of the communist-led Soviet Union. The safest way to protect the United States, they argue, is to have the strongest armed force in the world. One that can retaliate with such widespread destruction, no country will dare attack.

Convinced by people like McCarthy that they can be bombed off the face of the Earth if they don't have the capability to end all human life, the American people begin sacrificing the advances in health, education, and welfare being made in other countries to engage in an arms race with the Soviet Union to see which country will drive the other into bankruptcy first.

This is why the impact of Senator McCarthy's announcement about communists in the State Department reaches far beyond Ohio County Women Republicans. Like the Puritans who feared the Massasoits lurking in the woods outside of Salem, the American people had thought the danger represented by communism was from without. Now they're being told it also comes from within. And what are they going to do about it? Like the Puritans who discovered the witches in their community, they're going to panic. Fast. Through their representatives in Washington, they will give McCarthy in the Senate and the House Un-American Activities Committee in the Congress sweeping powers to conduct "witch hunts" of their own. Anyone suspected of being a communist or having anything to do with communism will soon be in danger of being summoned before the HUAC to confess his or her involvement and provide the names of others who've come under the spell of this evil ideology.

To testify before the committee will be said to be

"patriotic"; to choose not to answer the committee's questions will be said to be "guilty"; to name people suspected of communist sympathies will be said to be "sincere"; to refuse to name names will be said to be "trying to hide something." But communists, former communists, suspected communists, and even once-thought-about-being communists won't be the committee's only victims. Many Americans whose political views happen to be at odds with those held by the powers that be will have their income taxes audited, find themselves out of work, and be shunned by the people where they live. And that's just for starters. For some, the pressure becomes so great they kill themselves. No matter how you cut it, the committee wins. But does America?

Miller read about the Salem witch trials when he was a student at the University of Michigan, but he didn't think of writing about them until he heard the word "witch hunt" used to describe the activities of Senator McCarthy and the HUAC. The committee summoned "witnesses" to say what they knew about the existence of communism where they lived and worked. Once before the committee, the witnesses were bombarded with so many questions it was a wonder they could think straight, let alone answer with any degree of accuracy. Not that it mattered. Any statement that reinforced the fear of a communist threat was regarded by the committee as true and, with the help of television, spread like wildfire across the country.

Miller could hardly believe what was happening. That the planned terror of a few people could be acted upon so quickly and achieved so easily seemed almost evil to Miller. Especially when his cowardly friends started avoiding him and the phone stopped ringing with offers to produce his works. How could people who knew him personally and in some cases supposedly loved him be compromised so willingly? Had they no consciences? Or were they so frightened they were willing to hand over their consciences to the HUAC without weighing the consequences? Didn't they realize that in shunning him they'd become the tools of the country's conservative right wing? Didn't they realize they were also its victims? Who was worse: the cynical demagogues in government, business, and industry, or the ordinary men and women who decided not to accept their moral responsibilities?

These were the questions that Miller thought needed to be answered in a play. Not a play about the hearings in Washington—no one would be foolish enough to produce a direct criticism of the government when so much of the nation supported the HUAC's agenda—but one about the witch trials of 1692. Miller could write about the effects of mass hysteria on ordinary men and women, the prolongation of fear by people who saw in the witch hunts opportunities for their own gain, and the unnecessary loss of life that resulted from accusations made with no basis in evidence. Theatergoers could then draw their own connections between seventeenth-century Salem and what was taking place in the United States.

In 1952, Miller went to Massachusetts to examine the records of what occurred in Salem more than three hundred years ago. He read about John Proctor, Abigail Williams, Rebecca Nurse, Giles Corey, and all the other characters who would eventually show up in his play. And what they say in *The Crucible* is pretty close to what they said in court in 1692. Miller's problem was that he didn't have a story line to connect the people he wanted to write about. Without some kind of suspense or dramatic tension, he knew he couldn't write a successful play no matter how interesting the material.

Miller found what he was looking for when he learned that Abigail Williams accused Elizabeth Proctor of being a witch but refused to implicate her husband. In fact, Abigail seemed to go out of her way to protect John

Proctor. Miller asked himself why she would do that. What could Abigail have against Elizabeth? Could there be something going on between Abigail and John? Not likely. Abigail was only eleven, and John was sixty.

But what if Abigail was seventeen, and John was in his thirties—old enough to be married and have a few kids but still young enough to attract an impressionable, romantic young girl like Abigail. And what if Abigail was a maid in the Proctor house and Elizabeth got sick and John and Abigail found themselves doing a lot of chores together and one thing led to another and they became lovers and Elizabeth found out about it and made John fire Abigail and . . . You can see how Miller's mind worked. Let's take a look at how his imagination plays itself out in the text.

Chapter 2

The Characters

John Proctor

JOHN PROCTOR IS THE MOST MODERN Puritan in all of American literature. Handsome, rugged, and individualistic, he has no patience with hypocrisy, no time for fools, and no respect for people who wield power. He's also troubled. More than seven months before the action of the play begins, he had an affair with Abigail Williams. He feels guilty about what he did, but he also still has lustful feelings for his former servant girl.

We see one extent of Proctor's desire when he enters a room where Abigail and three of her friends are upset over the Reverend Samuel Parris's having caught them conjuring spirits in the woods outside of Salem. Abigail has just threatened to punish any girl who admits to committing a sin worse than dancing when Proctor appears in the doorway.

After sending two of the friends on their way, Proctor implies an appreciation of Abigail's ability to bewitch and flirtatiously asks his former lover about the rumors of witchcraft circulating in the town. Abigail puts Proctor's mind to rest about there being any witches in Salem and almost in the same breath expresses her still-strong desire for him. Proctor tells the girl to put such thoughts out of her mind. What's this? A minute ago, he was coming on to her with an innuendo about her being "wicked"; now he's telling her to behave herself? Abigail is understandably surprised, then angry, and finally reduced to tears, but Proctor is unyielding.

The former lovers are interrupted by several people from the town. Reverend Parris and Mr. and Mrs. Putnam

THE MOVIE VERSION OF *THE CRUCIBLE*, STARRING
WINONA RYDER AND DANIEL DAY-LEWIS, WON BOTH
CRITICAL PLAUDITS AND A HUGE AUDIENCE.

suspect the devil is at hand. Their daughters have been in and out of consciousness since they were discovered in the woods with Abigail and her friends. Parris is afraid his enemies will use his daughter's affliction to undermine his authority in the church, and the Putnams fear they will lose their only surviving child. Intelligent, respected, seventy-two-year-old Rebecca Nurse, who has seen her own eleven children and twenty-six grandchildren "through their silly seasons," offers some reasonable explanations for the children's behavior and predicts they will soon tire of their "mischief," but hysteria has already taken root: Mr. Putnam fears many children in the village will soon die, Mrs. Putnam has lost confidence in doctors as well as prayer, and Parris has sent for the Reverend John Hale from Beverly to investigate the possibility of witchcraft.

When Proctor enters this debate on the side of what's sensible, we learn more about him and the role he plays in the community. In short, he's a threat to those in power. His thinking is unconventional for his time, and his behavior is subversive. He doesn't attend church as often as he's supposed to, has avoided baptizing his third child, and is skeptical of a pastor who talks more about hell than God. Nor is Proctor shy about criticizing Reverend Parris's desire to increase his salary and own the parish house. And he's also quick to point out that Parris sent for the Reverend Hale without consulting the church's wardens.

No sooner is Proctor finished with Parris then he starts in on Mr. Putnam. His sins are the same as Parris's: power and greed. When Putnam accuses him of belonging to a faction in the church that is bent on overthrowing those in authority, Proctor replies that he knows of no such party but intends to join it as soon as he discovers where and when it meets. Can you see how Miller is manipulating our perspective? He makes Proctor attractive by endowing him with contemporary ideals and attitudes that contrast sharply with the Puritan values of authority and acquisition.

So we know pretty early on that Miller wants us to like Proctor. He's straightforward, honest, and pulls no punches when it comes to addressing hypocrites. He's also far from perfect. But the way Miller presents him, some of his vices seem, if not exactly attractive, at least somewhat democratic, recognizable, and understandable. This is especially true when, eight days after his encounter with Parris and Putnam, we get to see Proctor sitting down to dinner with his wife Elizabeth. To say she's a little distant is an understatement. The woman is an emotional ice cube. It's small wonder why hot-blooded Proctor is drawn to passionate Abigail Williams.

But that was then, and this is now. Proctor has had his affair, confessed his sin, and wants to make up. He tries to please Elizabeth by complimenting her poor cooking and rhapsodizing about their walking in fields together, but she won't warm up. He cheated on her when she was ill, and she cannot forgive him. And now that Abigail is accusing people of being witches, fourteen women are in jail, the deputy governor is threatening to hang them if they don't confess to being in league with the devil, and John seems reluctant to tell the court what Abigail said to him about the girls only dancing when they were discovered in the woods, what other conclusion can Elizabeth draw than her husband is still in love with their former servant?

When Proctor lets it slip that he was momentarily alone with Abigail the last time he was in Salem, Elizabeth turns to leave the table, but her husband stops her. He feels guilty enough about what happened between him and Abigail and refuses to put up any longer with his wife's cold shoulders and suspicious eyes. When he accuses her of turning their home into a court, Elizabeth replies that it is the magistrate in his heart that judges him, not she.

Hmmmm. Do you think it is Proctor and not Elizabeth who is administering his punishment? Or do you think Proctor accuses his wife of being unforgiving and uncharitable so he won't have to look to himself for the reasons that led to his adultery? He has confessed his sin, but has he understood his behavior? Some critics say Proctor likes to reduce complex problems to simple black-and-white issues, that he is more comfortable with external conflict—his rejection of Abigail, his criticism of Parris and Putnam, his admonishment of Elizabeth—than internal strife. The complicated gray area—his continued attraction to Abigail and his reluctance to expose her to the court, his attempts to placate Elizabeth while deceiving her about being alone with his former lover—unnerves him. Do you think by projecting his own faults onto others—criticizing Abigail for throwing herself at him and reprimanding Elizabeth for turning away from him—Proctor has found a way to avoid looking at himself?

It's hard to tell at this point in the play, but life for the Proctors isn't going to get any less complicated. No sooner has John told his wife that her idea of justice would "freeze beer" than their servant Mary Warren enters the house with a rag doll she made for Elizabeth. Having stopped himself earlier from criticizing his wife for letting Mary go to Salem after he forbade it, Proctor now vents his pent-up anger on the disobedient girl. He grabs her by her cloak and threatens to whip her if she ever leaves the house again. But instead of resisting him as she usually does, Mary goes limp. When she says she's been made sick by the court proceedings, Proctor's anger turns to curiosity and later dismay as he discovers the number of women accused of witchcraft has jumped from fourteen to thirty-nine.

And that's not all: Judge Hathorne has sentenced half-witted Goody Osburn to hang. He also sentenced homeless Sarah Good, but she managed to save herself from the gallows when she confessed to signing with her own blood a compact to help the devil overthrow God. Husbandless, pipe-smoking, sixty-year-old Goody Good was also sentenced, but she was able to have her hanging postponed until she gives birth to the child she claims she is carrying. Mary Warren, as might be expected of an uneducated, misinformed seventeen-year-old, sees the sparing of Sarah Good's life and the postponing of Goody Good's hanging not as examples of those in authority preying upon the weakest members of the community and turning them into scapegoats but as signs of the court's integrity and compassion.

Almost as disturbing for Proctor as Mary's high opinion of the magistrates is her announcement that as an official of the court she will have to leave the house every day to assist with God's work in Salem. Proctor reaches for his whip to teach the girl a lesson about where, when, and for whom she'll work, but before he can strike, Mary announces she saved Elizabeth's life by testifying in court that she never saw her mistress send out her spirit on anyone. Elizabeth send out her spirit? Proctor demands to know who made this charge. Mary is forbidden by law to say, but she doesn't have to. And Elizabeth knows the charges brought against her won't stay dropped for long. Abigail Williams wants her dead so John will be free to marry her.

In Elizabeth's mind, there's only one thing to do: John must discredit Abigail's testimony by exposing her as a whore. This, of course, also means exposing himself as an adulterer, and John is reluctant to cast himself as a sinner after being so high-mindedly critical of people like Parris and Putnam. It's one thing to admit his failings to his wife in the privacy of their home; it's quite another to admit them publicly in a community with which he has so often been at odds. Also, Proctor still cares for Abigail and doesn't want her to be hurt any more than she already has been by his rejection. When Elizabeth confronts him with this truth, he agrees to expose their former servant's lies to the court, but the Reverend Hale arrives before he can leave.

Forty-year-old John Hale is an authority on witch-craft, but his knowledge comes mostly from books. Salem is his first real case. Because he doesn't know anyone in the town and can't make sense of much of what he sees going on in the court, Hale has taken it upon himself to conduct his own investigation. On this night, he's visiting the homes of those who might be summoned. Elizabeth Proctor is the person he came to examine at the Proctor homestead, but it's her husband who is nervous. He says he has no fear of any questions the reverend might ask, yet lies about the number of times and the reason why he's missed so many Sunday services. He also claims to say his prayers, yet admits he hasn't had his third son baptized because he has no respect for a pastor whom he perceives to work harder at saving money than saving souls. Hale wonders if this is the right attitude for a man who professes to love God.

In an attempt to rescue her husband from the complicated gray area quickly rising around him, Elizabeth argues that John's poor opinion of Reverend Parris doesn't mean the devil resides in their home. Hale concedes her point, then changes his approach. He asks Proctor to recite the "Ten Commandments." Knowing that Sarah Good was sentenced to hang after she failed to remember them in court, Proctor begins to sweat. He struggles through nine but needs Elizabeth to help him with the one he can't remember: the one about adultery.

Not knowing about guilt-ridden Proctor's affair with Abigail and concluding that his inability to remember the commandment is an accurate measurement of his Christian character, Hale makes ready to leave, but he's stopped by something Elizabeth says to her husband: "I think you must tell him, John." Proctor reluctantly tells Hale what Abigail said about the children dancing in the woods and their sicknesses having nothing to do with witchcraft.

When Hale points out the number of people who've already confessed to conspiring with the devil, Proctor—now on surer footing in the landscape of the black and white—replies that some people will swear to anything if it will keep them from hanging. Hale recognizes the truth in this statement, but he isn't sure that Proctor is a good enough Christian to make a reliable witness. He asks the man if he believes in witches. Knowing his answer is critical, John responds in a way he hopes will protect him from further suspicion. He says he will not deny there are witches if the Bible says they exist. Elizabeth is more forthcoming. She cannot believe in witches regardless of what the Bible says and suggests that Hale make better use of his time questioning Abigail.

Abigail Williams. She's been busy fainting and sticking a needle in her stomach and claiming she was stabbed by Elizabeth Proctor's spirit. When marshals from the court arrive to discover in the Proctor home that the doll Mary Warren gave Elizabeth has a needle stuck in it, they have all the proof they need to charge Elizabeth with witchcraft. Proctor tries to defend his wife by questioning why the possible motives of the accusers are never considered:

> Why do you never wonder if Parris be innocent, or Abigail? Is the accuser always holy now? Were they born this morning as clean as God's fingers?

> I'll tell you what's walking Salem— vengeance is walking in Salem. We are what we always were in Salem, but now the little crazy children are jangling the keys of the kingdom, and common vengeance writes the law!

> This warrant's vengeance! I'll not give my wife to vengeance!

But Proctor has no choice. He cannot prevent Elizabeth from being taken away in chains. Furious with the marshals for their shabby treatment of his wife and disgusted with Hale for not sharing with them his knowledge about Abigail's false testimony, Proctor moves menacingly toward Mary Warren. He demands that she accompany him to court and explain to the judge how she stuck the needle into the doll for safekeeping before giving it to Elizabeth, but Mary claims that testifying against Abigail would be like signing her own death warrant. And that's not all. If Proctor tries to protect his wife by exposing Abigail's lies in court, the former servant will accuse him of lechery.

The cat is out of the bag. Proctor's private sin is now a public affair. And his rejection of Abigail has led to the imprisonment of thirty-nine innocent women, the sentencing to death of at least two, and the arrest of his wife. To save them and restore peace to the community, Proctor realizes he can no longer hide behind his own shield of hypocrisy. His lost soul must now appear naked before the people of Salem and suffer ridicule from those for whom he has no respect. But what do you think he is more ashamed of: the deed or the exposure?

Proctor accuses Abigail before Deputy Governor Danforth of trying to murder his wife and calls on Mary to testify that the accusations she made along with the other girls are false, but Danforth is not so quick to believe the obviously distressed servant. When Mary says her fainting at the sight of spirits in court was pretense, he orders her to faint as proof of her ability to act. Mary proves that she cannot faint on command, but she refuses to change her story. Danforth then asks Abigail if the spirits she saw might be only illusions. She responds with a threat about his not being safe from the power of hell when a sudden wind appears to blow on her and her fellow accusers. They start to shiver and scream that they are freezing. When Proctor hears Danforth accuse Mary of sending her spirit out on the girls, he grabs Abigail by her hair, denounces her as a whore, and accuses her of seeking revenge against Elizabeth for dismissing her.

This brings everyone back to the kind of reality we're more familiar with. At least temporarily. Proctor confesses his affair with Abigail and insists that Elizabeth's only crime was to cast a harlot out of their home. To determine if Proctor is telling the truth, Danforth summons Elizabeth from her prison cell to ask if her husband ever committed the crime of lechery. Knowing the importance Proctor places on his reputation, Elizabeth lies. Danforth has heard all he needs to, but Hale isn't convinced. He understands it's only natural for a wife to place her husband's life above a lie, and suspecting there may be vengeance working its way through Abigail's testimony, he accuses the girl of making false statements.

Sensing the direction in which Hale wants to lead Danforth, Abigail claims Mary Warren's spirit has taken the form of a bird and is trying to stop her and the other accusers from doing God's work. Frightened by the frenzy that Abigail is so quickly able to generate among the girls, Mary denounces Proctor as the devil's man and accuses him of threatening to murder her if his wife hangs.

Who would have guessed? Proctor, who has confessed the sin he committed (adultery), is arrested for the crime he didn't (witchcraft). Elizabeth, who never lies and can free herself from prison simply by telling the truth, lies and is sent back to her cell. Hale, who has been summoned to investigate the possibility of witchcraft, reaches his conclusion that there are no witches in Salem and is ignored. Danforth, who is supposed to be above the hysteria that is overtaking Salem, has become its instrument. And Abigail, who seems to do nothing but lie, threaten, and manipulate, has become a saint. Joining her in a kind of Unholy Trinity are Parris, who has used the witch trials to discredit those in his parish who don't share his values, and Putnam, who has successfully aided in the prosecution of people whose land he covets.

Three months go by. Elizabeth has been discovered pregnant and her execution has been delayed. Twelve others are not so lucky as to be pregnant and not so hypocritical as to admit to being witches. They'd rather die than lie. Reverend Hale tries to convince the seventy-two people waiting their turn at the gallows to confess their covenants with the devil. What does it matter if they lie? They know they are not witches, and by saving their lives, they honor God by preserving the precious gift he has given them.

In an effort to save Proctor's life, Hale gets the court's permission to have Elizabeth speak to her husband the morning he is scheduled to hang. Elizabeth makes no attempt to convince John to lie, but she does accept partial responsibility for his adultery. Had she not been so cold, he might not have turned to another.

Proctor, who has been talking less and listening more during his time in prison, has thought about Hale's sensible argument. Life, however unfair, is better than death. Especially when your soul is already lost. But Proctor has another reason to live. His sense of respect for others. He would rather lie about being an agent of the devil than share the scaffold with a genuine martyr such as Rebecca Nurse. Isn't it better to be a one-time adulterer and live than be a complete fraud and die? Elizabeth will not influence her husband's decision, but she does say that whatever he chooses she knows him to be a good man.

Elizabeth's response is as good as a reprieve. Hearing Proctor's decision to confess, Hale, Danforth, and others rush with pen, ink, and paper into the dungeon where Proctor has been chained to a wall. After he dictates his confession, however, Proctor discovers Danforth's plan to post it on the church doors as an example for others to come forth. Danforth also expects Proctor to name the people he knows keep company with the devil. Proctor refuses. He claims that God knows his sins; there is no need to publicize them. Nor will he allow the court to use his confession to justify the deaths of others.

Why not? Because of his own sense of self-respect and the sense of integrity by which he believes he is known in the community. What he calls his "name." Having lost his soul when he made love with Abigail, his name is all that allows Proctor to sleep at night without guilt. He may have loved life enough to confess his sin, but he doesn't love it enough for his confession to be made public. His reputation, once more important than the truth, is now more important than life.

Do you agree? Is life without honor a fate worse than death? What would you do if you were in Proctor's position? Confess to the wrong sins and live, or live by the right truths and die? Though he may be more concerned with his reputation than we'd like to see in a hero, Proctor is not as terrible a person as he once thought. In his final hour, he is able to make peace with his wife, serve as a model for his sons, prevent innocents from being summoned by the court, and honor the integrity of the victims who chose to die rather than lie. He also proves that he's capable of acting morally in a climate of hysteria: he questions the legal system as a reliable instrument of justice, condemns capital punishment as reasonable solution to a community's problems, and asserts his will to judge for himself what he did right, what he did wrong, and who will determine if, when, and how he'll die. In choosing the gallows, Proctor restores his reputation and his sense of integrity.

Abigail Williams

Few literary characters have been called as many bad names and with such enthusiasm as Abigail Williams. Critics have labeled her a harlot, a whore, a slut, a strumpet, a demon, a home wrecker, a power monger, and more. She lusts, lies, cheats, steals, threatens, plots murders, manipulates authority, conjures witches, drinks blood, dances naked, resents respectable people, introduces children to the ways of the devil, and doesn't care how many people hang as long as she gets her way. Hell knoweth no fury like that of a woman scorned and now, thanks to Abigail, neither do we. The girl is a one-child faith-based terrorist organization, with fear and the hysteria it produces in Salem her most formidable weapon. Not only that, but she gets away with her crimes.

But if Proctor's vices—deceiving his wife, threatening to whip his servants, tactlessly criticizing the faults of others, and hypocritically being more concerned with his good name than his bad behavior—can be understood and sympathized with, why can't Abigail's?

WINONA RYDER MADE A STRONG IMPRESSION AS ABIGAIL WILLIAMS IN THE 1996 MOVIE OF *THE CRUCIBLE*.

Let's look at Abigail from a perspective not explored by many of Miller's critics. Abigail is seventeen years old when she works for the Proctors. She's a servant in their home and is treated as such. When Elizabeth Proctor becomes sick, she finds herself sharing chores with the woman's good-looking, sexually attractive husband.

But John Proctor is more than just a hunk. He loves nature and can wax poetic about the fields he likes to walk through. He has a skeptical mind, one that must be very appealing to someone in Abigail's position in the Salem power hierarchy. Something of a rebel, he doesn't go to church, refuses to baptize his son, criticizes the material ambitions of Reverend Parris, and ignores the alleged property rights of Mr. Putnam. As a farmer with his own land and income, Proctor is also a man of substance. He can afford to hire servants to work in his home. And unlike his wife, Proctor is not cold. He falls for Abigail and she for him. How could she not? She was probably a virgin when they met, believed what he said in the heat of passion, imagined herself having servants instead of being one, and saw herself as much better suited for John than Elizabeth.

But when Elizabeth discovers her husband and her servant are having an affair, Abigail is fired, her knight in shining armor doesn't rescue her, no one else will hire her, and she is forced to live with her narrow-minded, power-hungry, materialistic uncle. Reverend Parris is not only everything Proctor is not, he embodies many of the false values Proctor has taught her to hate. Abigail dared to love, and for that she's punished. And while she suffers the humiliation of having to live with her hypocritical uncle, the man she loves stares up at her window whenever he walks by and flirts with her when the two are alone. Obviously he still feels the same way about her seven months after their last roll in the hay, and just as obviously to her, the only thing standing between them and their living happily ever after is a woman who doesn't exactly turn him on. What's the poor child to do?

There's not much she can do. All the power is in the hands of the Proctors. Elizabeth can fire her, and John can avoid her, and because she is poor and an orphan, Abigail is expected to get on with her life as best she can. But Abigail is no more your typical, ordinary Puritan than Proctor is. She's not going to give up without a fight. Because she can't turn for help to any of the respectable people in Salem or even the God she has offended by sinning with a married man, Abigail explores one of the few resources available to someone in her position: she asks the slave Tituba to contact spirits of the dead to kill Elizabeth so she and John can be together. All's fair in love and war, right? And Abigail is both in love with John and at war with Elizabeth.

Listening to Tituba's tales, singing her spirituals, dancing in the woods, running naked in the night, and drinking animal blood also enable Abigail to continue to experience the senses of freedom, excitement, and physical pleasure—introduced to her by John—that come from breaking conventional taboos. When she and her rebellious friends are discovered by the Reverend Parris, however, Abigail responds like the child she is. She lies to her uncle about what she was doing in the woods, and when he and Hale balk at believing her, she accuses Tituba of conjuring spirits. Some of the girls who were also caught dancing insist on telling the truth, but Abigail threatens them with a "pointy reckoning" so terrible they'd wish they never saw the sun go down.

Just how innocent Abigail was when she and Proctor met, how vulnerable she remains, how hurt she is by his subsequent rejection, and how driven she is to have him to herself become apparent when she sees her lover for the first time since Elizabeth dismissed her. His very presence excites the girl. When he admiringly predicts her unconventional behavior is going to land her in the stocks—a common form of public punishment at the time—before she's twenty, she takes his flirtatious approval to heart, grabs his hand, and proclaims her love for him. Proctor tells the girl they're through, but Abigail tearfully and correctly points out that anyone who held her the way John did when they made love, looked as he did when Elizabeth put her out, and burns with a loneliness that drives him to stand under her window on wintry nights, still desires her.

When Proctor tells Abigail that what they shared never happened, the girl's pain turns to anger. The knowledge he taught her was more than carnal. He opened her eyes to the hypocrisy in the community and is now hypocritically trying to close them as if nothing between the girl and her former employer had ever taken place. In tears, she tells him:

> I look for John Proctor that took me from my sleep and put knowledge in my heart! I never knew what pretense Salem was, I never knew the lying lessons I was taught by all these Christian women and their covenanted men!
>
> And now you bid me tear the light out of my eyes? I will not, I cannot! You loved me, John Proctor, and whatever sin it is, you love me yet. John, pity me, pity me.

These desperate words are the last Abigail speaks to Proctor, but he doesn't heed them, and the events set in motion by their affair spin out of control: a child tries to fly out a window, another slips in and out of consciousness, Mr. Putnam measures the worth of his neighbors' property, and Mrs. Putnam blames the deaths of seven of her children on good Rebecca Nurse. Under Parris's and Hale's heated barrage of questions about witchcraft,

Abigail blames the slave Tituba for all that has happened. Tituba denies the accusations, but what weight does the word of a slave carry against that of Abigail? It's either confess or die. When Parris and Hale rush to praise Tituba for revealing her pact with the devil, an inspired Abigail announces her love for God and starts naming the people she saw walking with the devil.

Abigail's behavior—her making love with Proctor, her plotting to be his wife, her conjuring spirits, her lying to Parris and Hale, and her denouncing others—reflect her age, but she also reveals an uncanny ability to size up situations, strategize outcomes, and act in what she sees as her own best interests. When she falsely accuses others of witchcraft, she almost instantly goes from being a sinner to a saint. And with her newly elevated status comes a power the former servant girl has never known. She no longer has to be afraid of being poor or whipped or thrown in the stocks. Abigail can intimidate those in authority, frighten those who threaten to betray her, and for the first time in her own life, have some control over her fate.

But such unrestricted power in the hands of an immature, emotionally charged, pathetically deluded girl is dangerous, especially when combined with someone of Abigail's intelligence and insight. With cold calculation, she selects for her first victims the old, drunk, homeless, and scatterbrained people she knows the majority of Salemites are critical of and predisposed to condemn. Every self-induced fit and accusation increases her authority, and every arrest and conviction increases her power. It isn't long before she gets caught up in the hysteria she has created. She no longer cares if innocent people die, because like a lot of obsessed people with enormous amounts of power, she doesn't see her victims as people. They are only instruments for protecting herself and furthering her goal to wed Proctor.

Abigail's thinking may be irrational, but her emotions are real, and so is the fear of witchcraft she creates in the community. When Deputy Governor Danforth asks her if her spirits might be illusions, the girl calls up a cold wind that sends shivers through her army of fellow accusers; when Mary Warren testifies against her, Abigail sees her antagonist's spirit in the form of a menacing yellow bird about to descend on those doing God's work; and when those in authority prove incapable of responding rationally to the hysteria that holds Salem in its grip, the former servant uses them to subvert the law and ensure that justice will not be done.

But when Abigail sees that her game is up, she runs away with her uncle's savings—another means to another end—as coolly as she plotted to kill Elizabeth Proctor. And as for John Proctor, he's history. If he wasn't, she wouldn't have told Mary Warren of her plan to accuse him of lechery.

Thanks to Abigail Williams, Salem will never be the same. But would the witch hunt she created have been possible if the community's social order had not already been out of balance? Didn't Reverend Parris's need for power, Mr. Putnam's desire for property, Mrs. Putnam's thirst for revenge, Elizabeth Proctor's coldness, John Proctor's lust, Deputy Governor Danforth's arrogance, Judge Hathorne's rush to judgment, Reverend Hale's loss of authority, Tituba's fear of death, and Mary Warren's fear of just about everybody also contribute? Could it be that the passion for killing that swept Salem was as much a product of its citizens' corrupt values as one girl's misguided vision of love? Could it be that a self-righteous social system can breed hysteria when the status quo is threatened by unconventional thinking and behavior? And could it be that witch hunts are inevitable in any community that's so absolutely certain of what's right and wrong?

The Sinners and The Saints

As he did in *Death of a Salesman*, Miller creates in *The Crucible* what writers call "reflector characters," people whose job is to reflect on the issues the main characters are trying to resolve. These reflector characters are almost always one-dimensional and rarely change their behavior. You could say they are dramatized points of view. In this play, the reflector characters are divided into two groups: the sinners (Reverend Parris and the Putnams) and the saints (Rebecca Nurse and Giles Corey).

Let's look at the sinners first. Reverend Parris is a materialistic paranoid who's more interested in power than prayer. Hell-bent on putting down anyone who opposes what he thinks is best for his parish, he alienates many in his congregation. They claim he talks more about the devil than God and is more interested in ownership of the rector's house, a free annual supply of wood, and golden candlesticks for his church than he is in saving souls.

Parris's most outspoken critic, John Proctor, not only stays away from services, he refuses to allow Parris to baptize his son. Rather than recognize his shortcomings, accept responsibility for his behavior, and improve his relationship with the people he's distanced from his congregation, Parris blames others for his unpopularity. His worst sin is when he sends for Reverend Hale, not so much because he wants his stricken daughter to get better, but because he fears his enemies in the parish will use the suspicion of witchcraft in his home as an opportunity to undermine his credibility as a man of God. Later, at the court hearings, Parris will continually argue in favor of his own self-interest regardless of which side he takes on the issue of hanging. Is it any wonder he leaves his house one morning to discover a knife stuck in the door?

Mr. and Mrs. Putnam are both greedy and spiteful. Mr. Putnam cynically uses the law to steal his neighbors' land, and Mrs. Putnam demonstrates a complete absence of conscience when she vindictively blames the deaths of seven of her eight children on Nurse for no reason other than the good woman has a large and healthy family. Thanks to Mrs. Putnam, Nurse is hanged.

Now for the saints. Rebecca Nurse, whose house still stands in Salem, may be the most respected person in her community. She demonstrates why when she refuses to save her life by confessing to a sin she hasn't committed. She knows that if she says she's a witch, she's also saying she's a hypocrite. People will think she pretended to be decent and respectable, but all the time she was really a liar and a fraud. Rebecca goes to her death so admired, John Proctor doesn't feel worthy enough to swing above the same gallows.

Eighty-three-year-old Giles Corey is an honest and likeable crank. On the basis of something said to him by a neighbor, he testifies that Mr. Putnam instructed his daughter to accuse George Jacob of witchcraft so the Putnams could acquire the innocent man's land after he was hanged. When Deputy Governor Danforth demands to know the name of the person who made this accusation, Corey refuses to say because he fears the man will wind up in jail, and he doesn't want to risk losing his land. Judge Hathorne finds Corey in contempt of court and orders that an increasing number of stones be placed on his chest until he says who it was that told him Putnam was trying to kill George Jacobs. Corey's final words are, "More weight."

Rebecca Nurse and Giles Corey are examples of two different kinds of virtues: the former won't lie to save her life; the latter would rather die than betray a confidence. Their goodness, however, is no match for the evil generated by Parris and the Putnams. Why do you think this is? And where do you think Rebecca and Giles learned that to give up their personal integrity is to become a real witch? Do you think they made the right decisions? Would you ever do what they did?

The Judges

The obvious judges are Hathorne, an ancestor of the writer Nathaniel Hawthorne, and Danforth; the not-so-obvious judges are Elizabeth Proctor and Reverend John Hale. The job of Hathorne and Danforth is to correct individual wrongs so the community's status quo can remain unchanged. They impress us as cold, hard, and cruel (Miller doesn't even tell us their first names), but they have a heavy responsibility and a huge challenge. They know their decisions are equated with what the people of Salem would call a moral right, and yet they have to base their decisions on the kinds of evidence they aren't used to handling.

Not only is much of the evidence circumstantial, the testimony of the witnesses is given in such an intense climate of hysteria that the judges soon get swept away by it despite their efforts to remain objective. Once they've been corrupted by their inability to distinguish between reality and illusion, they start acting to preserve their own power. When this happens, the innocent can no longer rely on the court to protect them, and any hope for justice is reduced to wishful thinking.

Hathorne and Danforth present themselves as confident, authoritative, and remorseless. When Giles Corey bursts in on the court with evidence he hopes will save his wife's life, Hathorne has him removed to the vestry where Danforth orders him to submit his evidence in a proper affidavit. When Francis Nurse claims the people accusing his wife Rebecca of witchcraft are lying, Hathorne wants the man held in contempt of court.

Danforth refuses to accept depositions, accuses John Proctor of conspiring to overthrow the court's authority, orders the arrests of the ninety-one people who signed a petition testifying to the good characters of the people sentenced to be hanged, charges Giles to reveal the name of the person who told him Mr. Putnam is murdering people for their land, warns Mary Warren about lying in court, silences Parris's attempts to influence the hearings, censures Reverend Hale for questioning the guilt of those already condemned to die, and tells the girls who've been accused of giving false testimony that he will not tolerate anything less than the truth. All of these actions are designed to instill confidence in the way the court proceedings are conducted. There will be no chaos in Salem because there will be no reason for chaos. Not with Hathorne and Danforth in charge.

But nothing in the careers of these two men has prepared them for the likes of Abigail Williams. She refutes the charges brought against her, accuses the court of mistrusting her, and threatens Danforth with the power of hell. Before the deputy governor can respond, Abigail summons a wind that makes her fellow accusers shiver. Danforth understands the unsettling message she is sending him, but he's still willing to adhere to procedure and grant Proctor his due right to testify. After John confesses his lechery, the deputy governor should question Abigail, but already unnerved by the power he thinks she commands, he calls instead on Elizabeth to confirm her husband's story.

The honest woman lies, and Danforth accepts her word as proof. He then rejects Proctor's and Hale's claim that Elizabeth is understandably trying to protect her husband's reputation. Common sense is not evidence. And neither is hallucination. Nevertheless, Danforth is willing to believe Abigail's vision of Mary Warren's spirit in the form of a yellow bird about to attack those doing God's work. He's also horrified by it. So is Mary Warren. When Danforth orders her to draw back her spirit, she recants her testimony that the girls are lying, pledges never to hurt Abigail again, and denounces Proctor as the devil's man. Hale claims the girl has gone wild, and Proctor—so angry he is almost beyond speech—announces that God is dead.

Desperate to stop the court from spinning out of his control, the deputy governor doesn't realize he is already out of control. He believed what he didn't see (the yellow bird) and refused to consider what he should have been able to understand (a woman trying to save her husband's life). He didn't believe Proctor and Mary Warren when they told the truth but believed Elizabeth and Abigail when they lied. Too distraught to listen to Hale's voice of reason in the orgy of falsehoods and hysterics that sweep the court, Danforth concludes that the accused girls are telling the truth and orders Proctor taken to jail.

Now that Danforth has determined Proctor is in league with the Antichrist, nothing short of a confession will save the farmer from the gallows. Neither he nor anyone else. When Parris tells Danforth that Abigail has fled Salem, the deputy governor refuses to consider if the girl's accusations may be false. Hale pleads with Danforth to pardon those awaiting execution because they won't confess to something they didn't do, but he refuses on the grounds that a pardon would be unfair to the twelve people already hanged. And to so much as postpone a single scheduled hanging would run the risk of casting doubt on the guilt of those who have been executed.

Orphans are going from house to house, cattle are wandering on the roads, crops are rotting in the fields, and those not waiting to be tried or die are walking around afraid that they will soon be summoned, but Danforth will not question whether he may have made a mistake. To have made a mistake (read: twelve mistakes and counting) will call into question whether he is fit to serve as deputy governor. Once Danforth's own self-interest becomes more important than any single person's innocence, we see how easily justice can be corrupted and fate controlled. Danforth is not a bad devil, but he is a weak one, and the damage he does is enormous. Proctor is right when he tells the deputy governor he'll see him in hell: "God damns our kind especially, and we will burn, we will burn together."

Elizabeth Proctor is a defendant but she's also a judge. She rules on her husband's affair with Abigail and administers their punishment. Unemotional and impersonal, she acts like a judge, but like Hathorne and Danforth, cannot arrive at a fair decision because she sticks so closely to the letter of the law. She doesn't consider the human factor in her deliberations, only the evidence. Because she lacks the ability to understand, sympathize, and act mercifully, Elizabeth's private justice is as misguided as the public justice administered in Salem. Even after John Proctor admits his adultery and serves a penance of seven months, Elizabeth will neither forgive nor forget.

But this doesn't mean she doesn't love him. Or is not willing to compromise her own values to save his life. When called upon to testify on her husband's behalf, Elizabeth lies because she knows how much value John places on his reputation. You would think Elizabeth's lying would make her more aware of her own human frailty and be more charitable toward her husband, but there's no indication at this point in the play that she's reached that deep a level of self-understanding. When Hale begs her to convince John to confess a crime he didn't commit, she responds by accusing the reverend of mouthing the devil's argument.

Danforth then tells her, "I tell you true, woman, had I no proof of your unnatural life, your dry eyes now would be sufficient evidence that you delivered up your soul to Hell!" This gets her to agree to talk to John, but when he asks for her forgiveness, she says it is not hers to give. The only one who can forgive John is John. Then, in a sudden moment of self-enlightenment, Elizabeth accepts a share of the responsibility for his adultery: "It needs a cold wife to prompt lechery." Though reluctant to forgive himself, John immediately forgives his wife.

Do you notice how many people in this play are prone to make unyielding judgments of others? Hathorne and Danforth judge people with all the unfeeling arrogance of

the Old Testament God, and John and Elizabeth Proctor
are reluctant to consider human feelings in almost any
moral verdict. When justice forgets charity, Miller seems
to be telling us, the results can be disastrous. Elizabeth's
lack of charity toward John leads to John's lack of charity toward Elizabeth and Mary Warren. And do you
remember Abigail's final words to John? Three times she
asks him to pity her. Had he shown some compassion for
the girl half his age who is now out of work and has to
live with an uncle Proctor has taught her not to respect,
nineteen people and two dogs might have lived past 1692.

Reverend John Hale arrives from Beverly as a sort of
spiritual doctor, and he knows from the many books he
has read that superstition has nothing to do with science.
What he doesn't know is that his learned information is
mostly irrelevant in a place that is already beyond reason.
Like any good scholar, he's initially skeptical of the stories
he hears and rationally begins to investigate the possibility of witchcraft, but he is soon caught up in the kind of
hysterical climate that makes witch-hunting possible.

After Parris threatens to whip Tituba if she doesn't
confess her compact with the devil and Mr. Putnam says
she should be hanged, Hale puts into the poor slave's
mind the thoughts she needs to save herself: he will be
merciful if she confesses, the afflicted children will be
healed, the devil may have been accompanied by someone
she knows, and she has been selected by God to help
cleanse the village by naming the witches within it. When
Tituba provides a name put in her mouth by Mr. Putnam
and wins the praise of Mrs. Putnam after denouncing the
bitter woman's midwife, Abigail seizes the opportunity to
knock off Elizabeth Proctor. Betty Putnam awakens from
her unconscious state to condemn others, her father
thanks God, Hale announces the spell is broken, and the
three hitherto mostly ignored girls are suddenly among
the most powerful people in Salem.

Hale knows, however, that confessions and accusations prove nothing. So he continues his investigation by examining the people he knows will be summoned before the court. He soon discovers there are no witches in Salem. He can't prove it because the only evidence he has is common sense, and the court won't listen to reason because Hathorne and Danforth have seen the devil's work with their own irrational eyes. Not wanting more blood on his hands than is already there, Hale challenges the court to look at the motives behind the accusations, but he can't convince Danforth to listen to what he doesn't want to hear or even to believe what he doesn't see, namely, the fictitious yellow bird Abigail has created to descend on any accuser who contradicts her.

Hale denounces the proceedings of the court, and in a desperate attempt to save innocent lives, tries to convince those awaiting execution to confess. Isn't life on a false confession preferable to death on a false charge? Rebecca Nurse and Giles Corey don't think so. Spiritual and moral integrity are more valuable than life. And so is John Proctor's good name. When Hale fails to convince the fallen farmer to surrender to the unacceptable, Salem's one last spark of hope for justice is snuffed out.

Chapter 3

Narrative Strategies

IN ADDITION TO CREATING REFLECTOR CHARACTERS to help articulate the central concerns of his play, Miller punctuates his text with lengthy descriptions of some of the main characters. These are not stage directions but psychological profiles based on his research of what happened in Salem in 1692. Before Reverend Parris opens his mouth, for example, we read that there is "very little good to be said for him." Similarly, Miller tells us what to think of Mr. Putnam, John Proctor, Rebecca Nurse, Reverend Hale, and Giles Corey before they're given a chance to reveal anything about themselves.

These descriptions also contain historical information about the Puritan community as well as critical comments about its culture. Because this information is not available to audiences sitting in a theater, people reading the play often have a slightly different experience than those seeing it on stage. For this reason, some directors have created a narrator to provide the characters' backgrounds. What do you think of this decision? Do you like knowing about some of the characters before they say their lines? Or do you think interrupting the flow of the play to provide historical information might keep you from getting caught up in the action?

When Miller's characters do speak, their words and sentence constructions resemble that of the seventeenth-century colonists. "Spite only keeps me silent," John Proctor tell us. And, "It's hard to give the lie to dogs." Some critics say this language is archaic and too formal;

others say it may not be as direct or as conversational as contemporary speech, but it elevates the diction of the play to a level that is just about as close to poetry as prose can get. Critics who favor the seventeenth-century language claim the words give the characters a kind of eloquence and dignity. Their opponents say the language is just bad English. "I only hope you will not be so sarcastical no more," is a popular example. "It were a grand sneeze" is another. What do you think? Did the language of the characters slow you down to the point where you were distracted from the story? Or did the language bring you closer to the people who lived in Salem in 1692? What would have been the difference if Miller's characters spoke as we do today? Have you ever considered reintroducing into your everyday speech the words that were used in colonial times? How do you think your friends would react if you said you were only "sportin'" with them or you didn't "truck" with people who did drugs or you accused mean-spirited people of "breaking charity" and warned them of a "pointy reckoning"?

The title of the play is also a part of its narration. The word "crucible" has two meanings. A crucible is a metal container that can withstand very intense heat. If we think symbolically of Salem as this kind of vessel, we see a community that cannot take the heat generated by a witch hunt. It may survive the hysteria that carried nineteen people to the scaffold but not in the same form: the Puritans' theocratic rule of government is now history.

The second meaning of "crucible" is that of a very difficult, soul-searching test, and few of the people in Salem are able to pass the one created by the threat of witches. This threat provides opportunities for Parris to increase his power in the church, Putnam to grab more land in the community, and Abigail to get rid of the woman standing between her and John Proctor. The results are catastrophic.

Hathorne and Danforth fail to enforce the law in ways that are just; Rebecca Nurse, Giles Corey, and John Proctor die; Elizabeth Proctor is widowed with three children; and the Reverend Hale has to live the rest of his life with blood on his hands.

Chapter 4

Period Piece or Relevant Drama?

MILLER TELLS US HE WROTE *THE CRUCIBLE* because he wanted to draw a parallel between the witch hunts of 1692 and those of the House Un-American Activities Committee in the 1950s. The play strikes hard at these terrible events, but not every early reviewer was hit by Miller's analogy. Of the seven New York papers to run reviews in the days following the opening night perform-ance, only three mentioned any parallels between *The Crucible* and the HUAC. Nevertheless, the parallels turned out to be what captured the public imagination and what most people talked about when they discussed the play.

Depending on their political views, people tended to view Miller's analogy as either inaccurate or insightful. Eric Bentley, for example, criticized Miller for equating witches with communists: "The analogy . . . can be seen as complete only to communists, for only to them is the menace of communism as fictitious as the menace of witches. The non-communist will look for certain reserva-tions and provisos. In *The Crucible*, there are none." Robert Warshon, on the other hand, commends Miller for equating the fiction of witches with the supposed threat of communism: "He has set forth brilliantly and coura-geously what has been weighing on all our minds; at last someone has had the courage to answer Senator McCarthy."

Debating the Question: Period Piece or Relevant Drama?

Mr. Miller's piece says that witch-hunting is still among the most popular of American pastimes, and that there is almost no charge too preposterous to be believed by even the most upright pillars of society. The parallel may seem a little strained at times, since the credulity and superstition of our New England ancestors clearly exceed our own powers of imagination . . .

—Wolcott Gibbs

Perhaps the proper way to judge Arthur Miller's play, *The Crucible*, would be to see it out of context—out of the persistent, and thus painful, and thus perhaps distorting setting of today. While watching, I tried to do this . . . and so I am driven to believe the evaluations of both tragic periods charged the lines with a power they would have missed had Mr. Miller visited the Salem Courthouse in a more tranquil time.

—Freda Kirchwey

It may be wholly true that what are currently referred to as political witch hunts now and then proceed from mass hysteria and are grounded in fear, and also that they are sometimes cruel, irresponsible, and deplorable . . . but there is considerable difference between persecution based on ignorant superstition and prosecution, however extremely and at times eccentrically conducted, in time of national peril.

—George Jean Nathan

Miller observes the tremendous force that mere accusation had at the time, something was evident as well in the McCarthy witch-hunts. A man's career could be ruined if he were merely asked, "Are you now or have you ever been a member of the Communist party?"

—Wolcott Gibbs

The subject is especially interesting today because of a few parallels to McCarthyism and because of our interest in abnormal psychology. . . . When one remembers the "invisible" nature of the crimes charged, the use of confessed conspirators against defendants who insist on their own innocence, then the analogy to McCarthyism seems quite valid.

—Paul West

I saw accepted the notion that conscience was no longer a private matter but one of state administration. I saw men handing conscience to other men and thanking other men for the opportunity of doing so.

—Arthur Miller

It was not only the rise of "McCarthyism" that moved me but something which seemed much more weird and mysterious. It was the fact that a political, objective, knowledgeable campaign from the Far Right was capable of creating not only a terror, but a new subjective reality, a veritable mystique which was gradually assuming even a holy resonance . . . . The terror in these people was being knowingly planned and consciously engineered, and yet, all they knew was terror. That so interior a subject and emotion could have been so manifestly created from without was a marvel to me. It underlines every word in *The Crucible*.

—Arthur Miller

The parallels today in the tensions created by totalitarian powers, actual and incipient, being apparent, Miller has shrewdly been content merely to indicate them, and so he corroborates our awareness of the paralysis of fear obsessing the authorities and intimidating our citizenry. Meanwhile, hysteria settles in, and its artificially generated recurrence establishes a native climate where the basic imbalance becomes the norm: license supersedes liberty, unbridled prejudice, intolerance, and bigotry gain control, and freedom's wings are clipped. Truly, now as then, the devil is in town.

—William H. Beyer

I am not pressing an historical allegory here. . . . Some might have equated the Indians with Russians and the local witches with Communists. My intent and interest is wider and I think deeper than this. From my first acquaintance with the story, I was struck hard by the breathtaking heroism of certain of the victims who displayed an almost frightening personal integrity.

—Arthur Miller

There was no response to McCarthyism, except for *The Crucible*. And when I was attacked, I was never defended. I think that's unforgivable.

—Arthur Miller

While controversy often results in an increase in ticket sales (think of Michael Moore's *Fahrenheit 9/11*), it had the opposite effect on Miller's play. People stayed away from the theater in which it was playing. They feared their attendance would be interpreted by everyone from friends to neighbors to colleagues as support for Miller's position. And the fact that they had to cross a picket line of anti-communist protestors didn't help. Nor did the rumor that government agents had been planted among the protestors to record who was entering and leaving the theater. Having your income taxes audited or getting fired from your job or being denounced in your community as a "commie-pinko" just wasn't worth the price of admission. *The Crucible* won the Tony Award for Best Play and ran for nearly six months, but it didn't last nearly as long as *Death of a Salesman*. Or even as long as its backers had hoped. When public support for the HUAC waned the following year, however, *The Crucible* was revived Off Broadway and ran for more than six hundred performances.

Miller has never allowed any doubt that he wrote the play in response to the McCarthy witch hunts, but is *The Crucible* limited to the injustices perpetrated by the HUAC? For a drama to live beyond the time in which it was written it has to speak to new audiences in new times, and *The Crucible* is now being produced in more theaters than ever. In 1996, it was made into a movie that stars Daniel Day-Lewis, who that same year married Miller's daughter Rebecca.

What do you think is the reason for *The Crucible*'s continued popularity? Is it more than just a story about one shocking incident and an important lesson about another? What does the play have to say to us today? Can you draw any parallels between Miller's drama and what you read in the newspaper, see on television, and talk about in your classes at school? Should religious beliefs have a bearing on political decisions? How big a role does religion play in our current government's agenda? Are there people in power exploiting crises to increase their ability to control events? Do you think not to support your government's policies is unpatriotic? What individual rights are you willing to sacrifice during a national emergency? Can you disagree with an action your government is taking and still be loyal to your country? Do you think people who disagree with those in power should be silenced or punished? How do you feel about people who are in prison without having been given their right to due process? What rights do you think should be taken away from prisoners as part of their punishment? What about those awaiting trial? What do you think when you learn that prisoners are being tortured and some even die while in American custody? Do you wonder how atrocities like this are allowed to happen in a democracy? What if those in power think their actions are morally right and those who speak out against them are either stupid or evil? Do you ever question whether people in authority can be trusted to act in the best interests of all? Do you think our country's current leaders would knowingly plan and consciously create a climate of fear? What purposes would it serve?

You can see from these questions that Miller's concerns extend beyond any particular time and place. His focus is on the ways ordinary people respond to the realities imposed upon them by those in power. Many of us, Miller seems to be saying, are too willing to resign our individual consciences in support of the decisions made by those in authority. Especially when these leaders equate their practices with what is morally correct. And the more extreme their behavior, the less willing we seem to be to object. We find ourselves proclaiming our belief in the freedom of speech but accepting the injustices committed against those who speak out against oppression. And when the never-ending battle between human rights and political terrorism is complicated by the fact that those who would limit dissent often claim they're protecting freedom, we easily become confused. We tend to side with those in power because we want to believe they are acting in the best interests of the country and its people. To think otherwise is almost unbearable because it means a trust has been violated, and there is probably very little we can do about it. Or rather we convince ourselves there is little we can do. In this sense, *The Crucible* serves as a testament and homage to those who choose to maintain their personal integrity rather than conform to an unjust status quo. It's also a warning. When we surrender our individual consciences to the agendas of witch hunters, we become witches ourselves. By not speaking out against oppression, we passively form our own pacts with the evil forces of our time, and rather than become part of the solution, we remain part of the problem.

Chronology

1915
Born on October 17 in Manhattan to Isidore and Augusta Miller.

1928
Moves with family to Brooklyn.

1932
Graduates from high school; works in an automobile parts warehouse.

1934
Enters University of Michigan School of Journalism.

1936
Transfers to the English Department, wins Hopwood Award at University of Michigan for *No Villain* (play).

1937
Wins Theatre Guild Bureau of New Plays award for *They Too Arise* and Hopwood Award for *Honors at Dawn* (play).

1938
Graduates with Bachelor of Arts from University of Michigan; writes radio plays for Federal Theatre Project.

1940
Marries Mary Grace Slattery. Publishes under the title *Situation Normal,* the journal he kept while conducting research for the film *The Story of GI Joe.*

1944
The Man Who Had All The Luck (play based on an unpublished novel).

1945
Focus (novel).

1947
All My Sons (play) produced; receives New York Drama Critics Circle Award.

1949
Death of a Salesman (play) produced; wins Antoinette Perry (Tony) Award, New York Drama Critics Circle Award, Pulitzer Prize; named "Outstanding Father of the Year."

1950
Adaptation of Ibsen's *An Enemy of the People* (play) produced.

1953
The Crucible; wins Antoinette Perry (Tony) Award and Donaldson Award for Best Drama.

1954
Denied passport for Belgian premiere of *The Crucible.*

1955
A View From the Bridge and *A Memory of Two Mondays* (one-act plays) produced; Youth Board of New York cancels Miller's scriptwriting contract because of his communist sympathies; divorces Mary Grace Slattery.

1956
Two-act version of *A View From the Bridge* opens in London; refuses to provide names of communists to House Un-American Activities Committee; awarded Honorary Doctor of Letters by University of Michigan; marries Marilyn Monroe.

1957
Found in contempt of Congress; *Arthur Miller's Collected Plays* published.

1958
Contempt charges overturned by United States Court of Appeals; elected to National Institute of Arts and Letters.

1959
Awarded Gold Medal for Drama by National Institute of Arts and Letters.

1960
The Misfits (screenplay) produced; *The Crucible* turned into an opera by Robert Ward; opera version of *A View From the Bridge* (Uno Sguardo dal Ponte) produced by Roberto Rossellini in Italy.

1961
Divorces Marilyn Monroe.

1962
Marries Ingeborg Morath; Marilyn Monroe dies.

1963
Daughter Rebecca born.

1964
After the Fall (commissioned for the new Lincoln Center Repertory Theater) and *Incident at Vichy* (plays) produced.

1965
Elected President of PEN (Poets, Essayists, and Novelists); holds office until 1969.

1967
I Don't Need You Anymore (short story collection) published.

1968
The Price (play) produced; serves as delegate to the Democratic National Convention in Chicago.

1969
Psychology and Arthur Miller (book-length interview) with Richard Evans; awarded Brandeis University Creative Arts Medal.

1971
The Portable Arthur Miller (plays, short stories, essays) published.

1972
The Creation of the World and Other Business (play) produced; serves as delegate to the Democratic National Convention in Miami.

1977
The Archbishop's Ceiling (play) produced.

1978
The Theater Essays of Arthur Miller published.

1980
The American Clock, (play adaptation of Studs Terkel's *Hard Times*) produced; *Playing for Time* (teleplay) produced.

1983
Directs *Death of a Salesman* in Beijing, The People's Republic of China.

1984
Salesman in Beijing (memoir) is published. Receives Kennedy Center Honor for lifetime achievement.

1987
Timebends: A Life (autobiography) published.

1991
The Ride Down Mt. Morgan (play) premieres in London, England.

1994
Broken Glass (play) produced; wins Laurence Olivier Award for Best Play in London (1995).

1996
The Crucible (screenplay) produced; receives Academy Award nomination.

1999
Fiftieth-anniversary production of *Death of a Salesman* on Broadway; wins Antoinette Perry (Tony) Award for Best Revival of a Play.

2000
The Ride Down Mt. Morgan and a revival of *The Price* appear on Broadway; major eighty-fifth birthday celebrations are held in the United States and England.

2002
The Crucible revived on Broadway; Arthur's wife Ingeborg Morath dies; *Resurrection Blues* (play) produced.

2003
Arthur's brother Kermit dies.

2004
Finishing the Picture (play) produced.

2005
Arthur Miller dies of congestive heart failure on February 10.

Major Works

Situation Normal (journal, 1940)
The Man Who Had All The Luck (play, 1944)
Focus (novel, 1945)
All My Sons (play, 1947)
Death of a Salesman (play, 1949)
An Enemy of the People (play, 1950)
The Crucible (play, 1953)
A View from the Bridge: Two One-Act Plays, includes
  A Memory of Two Mondays (1955)
A View from the Bridge: A Play in Two Acts (1956)
Arthur Miller's Collected Plays (1957)
The Misfits (screenplay, 1961)
After the Fall (play, 1964)
Incident at Vichy (play, 1964)
I Don't Need You Anymore (short stories, 1967)
The Price (play, 1968)
The Portable Arthur Miller (plays, short stories, essays,
  1971)
The Creation of the World and Other Business
  (play, 1972)
The Archbishop's Ceiling (play, 1977)
The Theatre Essays of Arthur Miller (1978)
The American Clock (play, 1980)
Playing for Time (teleplay, 1980)
Timebends: A Life (autobiography, 1987)

Other Works

No Villain (play, 1936)
They Too Arise (play, 1936)
Honors at Dawn (play, 1937)
The Grass Still Grows (revision of *They Too Arise* 1938)
The Great Disobedience (play, 1938)
Listen My Children with Norman Rosten (play, 1939)
The Golden Years (play, 1939)
The Half-Bridge (play, 1941)
"The Pussycat and the Expert Plumber Who Was a Man"
    (radio play, 1941)
"William Ireland's Confession" (radio play, 1942)
"The Four Freedoms" (radio play, 1942)
That They May Win (play, 1944)
"Grandpa and the Statue" (radio play, 1945)
"The Story of Gus" (radio play, 1947)
Jane's Blanket (children's story, 1963)
In Russia with Inge Morath (journal, 1969)
"Psychology and Arthur Miller" with Richard I. Evans
    (interview, 1969)
Fame (one-act play, 1970)
The Reason Why (one-act play, 1970)
In the Country with Inge Morath (journal, 1977)
Chinese Encounters with Inge Morath (journal, 1979)
Elegy for a Lady (play, 1982)
Some Kind of Love Story (play, 1982)
The Ride Down Mt. Morgan (play, 1991)
The Last Yankee (play, 1993)
Broken Glass (play, 1994)
Essays Down the Corridor (2000)
Resurrection Blues (play, 2003)
Finishing the Picture (play, 2004)

Screenplays

The Hook (unpublished 1951)
The Witches of Salem (1958)
The Misfits (1961)
The Crucible (1996)

Short Stories (a sampling)

"The Plaster Masks," *Encore: A Continuing Anthology* 9 (April 1946): 424–432.

"It Takes a Thief," *Collier's* 119 (8 Feb. 1947): 23, 75–76.

"Monte Saint Angelo," *Harper's* 202 (March 1951): 39–47.

"The Misfits," *Esquire* 48 (Oct. 1957): 158–166.

"I Don't Need You Anymore," *Esquire* 52 (Dec. 1959): 270–309.

"Please Don't Kill Anything," *Noble Savage* 1 (March 1960): 126–131.

"The Prophecy," *Esquire* 56 (Dec. 1961): 140, 268–287.

"Glimpse at a Jockey," *Noble Savage* 5 (Oct. 1962): 138–140.

"Search for a Future," *Saturday Evening Post* 239 (13 Aug. 1966): 64–68, 70.

Teleplay

Playing for Time (CBS, September 1980)

Articles

"Subsidized Theatre," *The New York Times*, June 22, 1947, II: 1.

"Tragedy and the Common Man," *The New York Times*, February 27, 1949, II: 1, 3.

"Arthur Miller on 'The Nature of Tragedy,'" *New York Herald Tribune*, March 27, 1949, V: 1, 2.

"Ibsen's Message for Today's World," *The New York Times*, December 24, 1950, II: 3, 4.

"The 'Salesman' Has a Birthday," *The New York Times*, February 5, 1950, II: 1, 3.

"A Modest Proposal for the Pacification of the Public Temper, *The Nation*, 179 (July 3, 1954): 5–8.

"The American Theatre," *Holiday* 17 (January 1955): 90–98, 101–102, 104.

"A Boy Grew in Brooklyn," *Holiday* 17 (March 1955): 54–55, 117, 119–120.

"The Family in Modern Drama," *Atlantic Monthly*, 197 (April 1956): 35–41.

"The Playwright and the Atomic World," *Colorado Quarterly* 5 (Autumn 1956): 117–137.

"Introduction," *Arthur Miller's Collected Plays* (New York: Viking, 1957): 3–55.

"The Writer in America," *Mainstream* 10 (July 1957): 43–46.
"The Shadows of the Gods," *Harper's* 217 (August 1958): 35–43.

"Bridge to a Savage World," *Esquire* 50 (October 1958): 185–190.

"My Wife Marilyn," *Life* 45 (22 December 1958): 146–147.

"The Bored and the Violent," *Harper's* 225 (November 1962): 50–52, 55–56.

"On Recognition," *Michigan Quarterly Review* 2 (Autumn 1963): 213–220.

"Our Guilt for the World's Evil," *The New York Times Magazine* (January 3, 1965): 10–11, 48.

"What Makes Plays Endure?" *The New York Times* (15 August 15, 1965): 1, 3.

"The Role of P.E.N.," *Saturday Review* 49 (June 4, 1966): 16–17.

"Literature and Mass Communication," *World Theatre* 15 (1966): 164–167.

"It Could Happen Here—And Did," *The New York Times* (April 30, 1967): Sec. II, 17.

"The Age of Abdication," *New York Times* (December 23, 1967): 22.

"The Contemporary Theatre," *Michigan Quarterly Review* 6 (Summer 1967): 153–163.

"On Creativity," *Playboy* 15 (December 1968): 139.

"Broadway From O'Neill to Now," *New York Times* (December 21, 1969): Sec II, 3, 7.

"The War Between Young and Old," *McCall's* 97 (July 1970): 32.

"Men and Words in Prison," *The New York Times* (October 16, 1971): 31.

"Arthur Miller on 'The Crucible,'" *Audience* 2 (July–August 1972): 46–47.

"The Measure of Things Is Man," *Theatre* 4 (1972): 96–97.

"Every Play Has a Purpose," *Dramatists Guild Quarterly* 15 (Winter 1979): 13–20.

Interviews

Henry Hewes, "Broadway Postscript: Arthur Miller and How He Went to the Devil," *Saturday Review* 36 (January 31, 1953): 24–26.

John Griffen and Alice Griffen, "Arthur Miller Discusses *The Crucible*," Theatre Arts 37, October 1953): 33–34.

"*Death of a Salesman*: A Symposium," *Tulane Drama Review* 2 (October 1958): 63–69.

Allan Seager, "The Creative Agony of Arthur Miller," *Esquire* 52 (October 1959): 123–126.

Henry Brandon, "The State of the Theatre," *Harper's* 201 (November 1960): 63–69.

Josh Greenfield, "'Writing Plays is Absolutely Senseless,' Arthur Miller Says, 'But I Love It. I Just Love It.'" *The New York Times Magazine* (February 13, 1972): 16–17, 34–39.

Further Information

Books

Arthur Miller. San Diego, CA: Gale Group, 1996.

Bloom, Harold. *Arthur Miller*. New York: Chelsea House, 1999.

————. *Arthur Miller's Death of a Salesman*. New York: Chelsea House, 1995.

Web Sites

"Arthur Miller's *Death of a Salesman*"
http://www.deathofasalesman.com

"Arthur Miller's *The Crucible: Fact & Fiction*"
http://www.ogram.org/17thc/crucible.shtml

Interview with Arthur Miller
http://www.deathofasalesman.com/am-interview.htm-

"The Crucible Project"
http://204.165.132.2:90/crucible/main3.htm

Films

Death of a Salesman (1986). Directed by Volker Schlondorff, with Dustin Hoffman.

The Crucible (1996). Directed by Nicholas Hytner, with Daniel Day-Lewis.

Bibliography

Bentley, Eric. "The Innocence of Arthur Miller" (16 February 1953) from *The Dramatic Event: American Chronicle* (1954). Reprinted in *Contemporary Literary Criticism*, 78, James P. Draper, ed. (Detroit, MI: Gale Research, 1994): 290–291.

Beyer, William H. "The State of the Theatre: The Devil at Large," *School and Society*, 77, No. 1966 (February 2, 1953): 183–186.

Bierman, Judah, James Hart, and Stanley Johnson. *The Dramatic Experience* (Englewood Cliffs, NJ: Prentice-Hall, 1958).

Bigsby, Christopher (ed.). *The Cambridge Companion to Arthur Miller* (Cambridge: Cambridge University, 1997).

Bloom, Harold (ed.). *Arthur Miller* (New York: Chelsea, 1987).

Brown, John Mason. "Even as You and I," *Saturday Review of Literature*, 32 (February 26, 1949): 30–32.

Carson, Neil. *Arthur Miller* (New York: St. Martin's, 1982).

Gibbs, Wolcott. "The Devil to Pay," *The New Yorker*, 27, 50 (January 31, 1953): 47–49.

Guiles, Fred. *Norma Jean* (New York: McGraw-Hill, 1969).

Hawkins, William. *"Death of a Salesman*: Powerful Tragedy," *The New York World-Telegram* (February 11, 1949): 16.

Helterman, Jeffrey. "Arthur Miller" in *Twentieth-Century American Dramatists*. John MacNicholas, ed. (Detroit, MI: Bruccoli Clark, 1981).

Hynes, Joseph. "Attention Must Be Paid," *College English*, 23 (April 1962): 574–578.

Kirchwey, Freda. "The Crucible," *The Nation*, 176, 6 (February 7, 1953): 131–132.

Levin, David. "Salem Witchcraft in Recent Fiction and Drama," *New England Quarterly*, (December 1955): 537–542.

McCarthy, Mary. "Naming Names: The Arthur Miller Case," in *Twentieth-Century American Literature*. Harold Bloom, ed. (New York: Chelsea, 1987).

Martine, James J. (ed.). *Critical Essays on Arthur Miller* (Boston: G. K. Hall, 1979).

Miller, Arthur. *Death of a Salesman* (New York: Viking, 1949, and Bantam, 1951; Harmondsworth: Penguin, 1961) and in Gerald Weales (ed.), Viking Critical Library Edition (New York: Viking, 1967; Harmondsworth: Penguin, 1977).

———. *The Crucible* (New York: Viking, 1953; Harmondsworth: Penguin, 1968) and in Gerald Weales (ed.), Viking Critical Library Edition (New York: Viking, 1971; Harmondsworth: Penguin, 1977).

Moss, Leonard. *Arthur Miller* (Boston: Twayne, 1967).

Nathan, George Jean. Untitled essay (1953). In *Contemporary Literary Criticism*, 78, James P. Draper, ed. (Detroit, MI: Gale Research, 1994): 295–296.

Porter, Thomas. "Acres of Diamonds: *Death of a Salesman.*" *Myth and Modern Drama* (1969). Reprinted in *Twentieth-Century American Literature*, Harold Bloom, ed. (New York: Chelsea House, 1987): 127–152.

Starkey, Marion. *The Devil in Massachusetts* (Garden City, NY: Doubleday, 1961).

Warshon, Robert. "The Liberal Conscience in *The Crucible*," *Immediate Experience* (New York: Doubleday, 1962).

West, Paul. "Arthur Miller & the Human Mice," *Hibbert Journal* (January, 1963): 84–86.

Zolotow, Maurice. "Re-enter Mr. Miller," *Marilyn Monroe*. Reprinted in *Twentieth-Century American Dramatists*, John MacNicholas, ed. (Detroit, MI: Bruccoli Clark, 1981).

Index

Page numbers in **boldface** are illustrations, tables, and charts. Fictional characters are shown with a (c).

About the Author

Richard Andersen is a former Fulbright Professor of American Literature, James Thurber Writer in Residence, and Karolyi Foundation Fellow. His twenty-two books include six books on writing, five novels, four critical studies of twentieth-century American authors, a biography, and *Arranging Deck Chairs on the Titanic*, an examination of the crises in contemporary education. *Getting Ahead*, a guide to successful career skills, has been translated into three languages. Springfield College, where Dr. Andersen teaches writing and literature, nominated him in 2003 for the Carnegie Foundation's United States Professor of the Year Award.